M000033743

## Feedback

Please send us your valued feedback through
our website: www.baliexpat.com

# Contents

4

# Disclaimer

# Introduction

With a low cost of living, warm weather, fascinating culture, friendly people and stunning scenery, it's not surprising that many foreigners are starting to take advantage of Indonesia's retirement program. Bali is the first choice for many foreigners, where it is possible to experience a unique and different culture, while still being able to find many of the comforts people are used to from their home country.

It is often said that living in Bali on a permanent basis, rather than just visiting for a holiday, is a completely different experience. There are of course both advantages and disadvantages to living in Bali on a full time basis, versus just coming for a holiday. Being able to stay in Bali for a longer period, allows you to make longer and deeper relationships with people and you have more time to get to know more of Bali first hand.

Typically when you are on holiday you want to make the most of your short vacation time and you are more likely to look over any mishaps. With the lower cost of most things like restaurants and massages, you'll have no trouble living it up a little when you are on holiday.

When you move to Bali initially it will feel like you are still on holiday. You will of course need to look for a more permanent place to stay than a hotel and start buying everything you need to make your life comfortable. This process is enjoyable for most people.

Sometime after you make the move, you can be sure that something will happen that will burst the holiday bubble. You might have a problem with a landlord, you might get something valuable stolen or you might be involved in a traffic accident. As a result of this, some people will start to question their decision to move to Bali. Most will be able to put the incident behind them, but you can be sure of one thing—you will start to realize that living in Bali is not the perfect paradise you may have imagined it to be.

Bali is a beautiful and relaxing place to live, but life can also feel at times to be quite busy or even hectic. I don't mean in the western nine-to-five sense, but there always seems to be something going on. Balinese have their own calendar to determine the dates of ceremonies, which is just 210 days long; so important ceremonies like Galungan always seem to be coming around.

How much you get involved personally with participating in Balinese ceremonies is up to you. Some foreigners, especially those that have Balinese partners, even convert to Hindu. Even if you prefer not to get involved with the ceremonies, they will still affect your life in Bali as friends and possibly your staff will be busy preparing for and attending them. On the day of Nyepi for example, you cannot leave your house except for medical emergencies and even the airport is closed. Even just running a house can sometimes feel like a full-time job, and if you employ staff to manage your house, you will still need to spend time directing and managing them.

Houses in Bali are built to different standards, perhaps due to the tropical climate, but something always seems to need fixing.

It is generally easy to make local and expat friends in Bali and depending on how social you want to be, you will probably spend a great deal of time meeting them. Balinese and Asian people in general don't seem to like being alone and sometimes you might feel the need to just get away, to have some time by yourself.

Particularly in the villages of Bali, friends and neighbors will sit around on the 'Bali Bengong' and just chat, rather than sitting around watching television. This is perhaps one of the reasons why Bali is a great place to retire to.

This guide is meant to provide practical information on retiring in Bali and give you as much information as possible about what it's like to live in Bali, including both the negative and positive aspects. Another aim of this guide is to try to help you to examine why you want to live in Bali and try to make sure you are making the move for all the right reasons so you will be a little more prepared, both physically and mentally when you make the eventual move. If you still have questions after reading this guide, please don't hesitate to contact me at: mike@baliexpat.com

# Why even retire overseas?

With the hassle of getting visas, being away from friends and family and having to communicate in a different language, you are sure to have some people around you who will question why you want to live overseas. It might be a good idea to look at some of the reasons why you might want to retire overseas. If you have a partner or if you are still raising a family, everyone will need to be in agreement on the move.

Moving to Bali doesn't necessarily have to be permanent. Some people might choose to keep a house in their home country and buy or rent a house overseas. With the discount flights that are available in the region, spending time in Bali and other fantastic places in Asia like Thailand or the Philippines is also a possibility.

Some of the reasons to retire overseas include:

1. The chance for an adventure
2. The opportunity to learn a new language
3. A new romance
4. Possible lower cost of living
5. The warmer weather
6. To help people less fortunate
7. To start a new business
8. To make new friends

You might want to make a list now of some of the reasons why you want to live overseas and discuss them with your partner and family.

# Alternative retirement destinations

While this guide is about retiring in Bali, I thought I would at least take a look at other countries that offer a retirement scheme. Some people who have bought this guide will have already decided that they want to live in Bali. For people who are sitting on the fence, I thought it would be good to compare some alternative destinations. Even if you have decided on Bali, this will give you some idea about what other locations have to offer.

If you are undecided, one way would be to try and spend some time in the countries that you might want to live in. That, however, might not be easy for some people. Many people reading this guide will be looking to pack up all of their belongings and ship them to their future retirement location.

Talking to other expats who have lived in that country is some help, but unless you have similar interests and personalities, your own feelings could be completely different. There are several websites and magazines that are dedicated to expat living and retiring overseas, but again, these can offer biased viewpoints.

Here are some of factors you might want to look into when researching possible countries:

1. Country infrastructure. Roads, internet, sewerage, water electricity
2. Cost of living
3. Medical care
4. Pollution
5. Visa situation
6. Language
7. Tax situation
8. Culture and religion

9. Ease of meeting people

10. Attractions and things to do

11. Climate

There are a number of websites and magazines that list and rank their top overseas retirement destinations, such as International Living. While these lists seem to be well researched, they are still very subjective. International Living's top retirement destinations are based on eight factors:

- Property – affordability of buying property

- Entertainment and culture

- Cost of living

- Safety and stability

- Healthcare

- Climate

- Special benefits – things like tax breaks and other benefits for expats

- Infrastructure

Here are their top 25 retirement destinations for 2010:

1. Ecuador

2. Panama

3. Mexico

4. France

5. Italy

6. Uruguay

7. Malta

8. Chile

9. Spain

10. Costa Rica

11. Brazil

12. Argentina

13. Colombia

14. New Zealand

15. U.S.

16. Portugal

17. Australia

18. Belize

19. Malaysia

20. Ireland

21. Nicaragua

22. U.K.

23. Honduras

24. Dom Rep

25. Thailand

Using their ranking factors, it's probably not surprising that Indonesia didn't even make it on the list! Indonesia's healthcare and general infrastructure is still underdeveloped and is generally having trouble meeting the demand of a rapidly growing population. Indonesia's neighbor, Malaysia, comes in at 19 and nearby Thailand, at 25. I don't think people reading this would be wholly concerned about these kinds of lists. The list seems to be dominated by South American countries, which are probably of more interest to people from the United States due to their close proximity.

I spent two years traveling around Asia, so wanted to give a brief introduction to a few other countries in the region that people might consider. Several countries in South and Central America, like Belize, Panama, Costa Rica offer similar opportunities for retirement and because of their proximity to the United States, they will continue to be popular with North Americans. Unfortunately, I haven't had a chance to travel to South America, so I will leave it to others to write about those countries.

So what is the attraction many people have to Southeast Asia? Southeast Asia has a warm tropical climate and offers expats a low cost of living. The local people are typically warm and friendly to westerners, and the food is some of the best and healthiest in the world.

With that said, let's take a closer look at some of the countries in the region.

Cambodia – Cambodia is kind of like the "wild west" of Asia and is well known for its Angkor Watt temple and the Killing Fields, where thousands of people were murdered under the Pol Pot regime. On a visit to the Killing Fields just outside of Phenom Penn, tour guides will offer a side trip to a shooting range where you can let off a few rounds with an AK47. And while Cambodia has a troubled history, you will always be greeted with a smiling face.

Cambodia has perhaps the most flexible visas in the Asia Pacific region. Basically you can get a business visa for one year which entitles you to work, holiday or do business. Cambodia is ranked 148 in the world in terms of GDP per capita, so it's a poor country and is still suffering from the affects of the Khmer Rouge. Cambodia's beaches are nice, but not as nice as neighboring Thailand in my opinion.

Sihanoukville is the main beach town and it's popular with tourists and expats. The capital, Phnom Penh, is a fairly laid back Asian city and Siem Reap is the home of Angkor Watt. Most expats living in Cambodia run their own business, teach English or work for an NGO.

Cambodia is one of Asia's cheapest countries to live in, but the level of infrastructure and medical care is not great.

<u>Laos</u> – Laos is a land-locked country located north of Thailand that also shares borders with Cambodia and China and is sometimes described as being like Thailand 20 years ago. It's a poor country that was heavily bombed during the Vietnam War, but it has some beautiful landscapes, and the people are very laid back and friendly.

Infrastructure, like the internet, is not great but adequate for most people's needs. While Laos might not have the shopping, medical and nightlife options of its neighboring Thailand, for people looking for a quiet and simple life away from the maddening crowds, Laos could be ideal.

Laos seems to have no problem with people staying indefinitely on tourist visas. Getting a new one means crossing the border into Thailand and back again to get a new stamp. There are also other long term visas available. The Retire Asia (www. retire-asia.com) website has an excellent summary of what it is like to live in Laos.

<u>Malaysia</u> – The Malaysian government is the only country in the region, that actively promotes itself as a place for expats to come and live and has a well regarded program which enables people to stay on a long term basis in the country. Malaysia is also one of the few countries in the region where foreigners can even own freehold property in the country.

Malaysia's expat program is called "My Second Home" or MM2H, where 10 year visas are available. You can even apply to get permission to work part-time. You can find more details about the program on the official government website: www.mm2h.gov.my

Malaysia's cultural mix of Malay, Indian and Chinese reflects the many eating options in the country. Eating out is definitely one of the joys of traveling to or living in Malaysia.

Malaysia's cost of living is probably cheaper than most western countries, but a little more expensive than neighboring Thailand and Indonesia. Infrastructure is generally very good, with an excellent road network and is not nearly as chaotic as in other countries in the region. Malaysia is also becoming a popular place for medical tourism, with excellent health care at a fraction of the cost that you would expect to pay in a western country.

With of all of those things going for the country, I sometimes wonder why many foreigners choose to live in the Philippines, Thailand or Indonesia over Malaysia, since the Philippines, Thailand and Indonesia are generally not as welcoming to foreigners who want to work or live permanently in their countries.

My own opinion is that it's not as easy to mix with the local people in Malaysia. I'm not saying you won't make friends in Malaysia, but it's not like Bali where there's a good chance you will eventually meet everyone in the village you are living in and you will have much more contact with the local people. Wealthier Malaysians and expats also tend to live in condos and 'gated communities' which are great from a safety perspective, but they can be more isolated.

The Philippines – Like Indonesia, the Philippines is made up of thousands of islands. The Philippines played host to several U.S. military bases which had a strong influence on the culture of the country. Most people speak English very well, and English is even an official language of the country along with Filipino.

A 60 day tourist visa is available to travel to the Philippines, which can then be renewed for another 60 days. You can keep renewing the tourist visa for up to 16 months before you then need to leave the country! The extension process is fairly straightforwad and can be done in one day.

A retirement visa is also available, where you'll need to deposit around US$50,000 with the government, but many people just stay on the tourist visa.

The United States has a strong influence on the Philippines and this is perhaps most evident by the large number of U.S. fast food franchises. One of the main criticisms people often have with the Philippines is that the food is not as good as the other countries in South East Asia.

Despite having many beautiful and interesting places to visit in the Philippines, tourism is not so widely developed if you compare it to a place like Thailand.

<u>Thailand</u> – Thailand has a retirement visa scheme for people of at least 50 years of age. Applicants need to show a minimum of 800,000 baht or about US$25,000 in their bank account, or the equivalent sum of money in a monthly pension.

Thailand is one of most popular tourist destinations in Asia. Thailand has a large expat population, living all over the country, with greater concentrations in the capital Bangkok and the island resort of Phuket.

Thailand and Bali have their similarities and you often see people comparing Thailand's islands like Phuket and Bali. You can now even fly direct between the two islands on discount airlines such as AirAsia.

I have found the food to be excellent and the people of Thailand to be warm and friendly. The beaches and islands in Thailand are some of the best in the region. Like Bali, Thailand's popularity and unchecked development is starting to have a heavy impact on the environment. The cost of living is very reasonable, but Thailand like Indonesia, has restrictions on foreigners buying freehold property in the country.

# Why Bali?

So if you are still reading this, it must mean you haven't been sidetracked by another country and still want to live in Bali! And if you haven't done so already, I would strongly suggest visiting Bali to get a good feel for the place. As with many beautiful travel destinations, the images used by travel agents and tourism boards are of gorgeous beaches, Bali's famous rice terraces, its temples and the beautiful smiling faces.

There's no doubt that Bali is a beautiful island and in my opinion it deserves the attention that it receives. You will see Bali being promoted as a 'tropical island paradise', and to a degree that's true. It is a tropical location and it's an island, but you will find many people arguing on expat forums over whether living in Bali equates to 'living in paradise'. The bottom line is paradise means different things to different people.

For avid surfers, scuba divers or *gamelan* enthusiasts, Bali could well be paradise for them. After spending three hours in a traffic jam, on a trip that should only take 20 minutes, you might start wondering what kind of 'paradise' living in Bali is. I've heard of people who have traveled the globe looking for the 'perfect paradise' only to discover after all of that searching, they came to the conclusion that paradise is a state of mind rather than a specific location. There is never going to be one perfect place to live. Everywhere in the world is going to have its positive and negative aspects; it's just a matter of finding a place where those positive aspects outweigh the negative ones.

## *The negatives*

Bali is far from a perfect place to live. Indonesia is still a developing country and ranks 119 in the world in terms of GDP per capita. (http://en.wikipedia.org/wiki/List_of_countries_by_GDP_(nominal)_per_c apita) According to the UN, nearly half of Indonesia's population of 220 million people lives on less than US$2 a day.

Having said that, currently Indonesia's economy is one of the strongest in the region, with strong exports in natural resources and rising tourism numbers. The problem is, the very wide gap between the rich and poor in the country. Bali contributes to around 45 percent of all Indonesia's tourism earnings, so most family's incomes in Bali are dependant in some way on the tourism industry.

Infrastructure

The huge success of Bali as a tourist destination is starting to cause problems on the island and needs to be addressed very soon. Bali's infrastructure is not coping well with the increase in new hotels and villas on the island. Despite high rainfall in Bali, there are no dams to hold water. Most houses tap into the ground water, and as more wells are dug, even the ground water is going to eventually start to dry out.

In addition to that, there are neither proper sewerage systems nor proper systems for rubbish removal. Many locals burn their rubbish, including plastic, or throw it into the rivers. There are movements to reduce the number of plastic bags used in Bali, but it is still taking time for people to become aware of this growing problem.

Cheap finance is putting more new cars and motorbikes on the roads every day. Bali's roads and limited highways were simply not built to support this huge increase in traffic. In the south of Bali traffic jams are becoming the norm in many areas, and even if the government had the budget to build new roads, there simply isn't the space.

Bali's economic growth has made it a popular place for people from other parts of Indonesia to move to and find work, further adding to the increase in population.

The growth is also putting a large strain on Indonesia's electricity. Towards the end of 2009, the power was cut once every two weeks in the evenings as maintenance was done on the generators.

I write about this not to try and put you off, but to give you a clearer picture of what life is like in Bali and what you can expect. For me personally, electricity and water shortages, makes me realize how important these resources are and not something we can just take for granted in any country.

If you want to move to a country that has a lower cost of living, you need to realize that you cannot expect everything to work like it did in your home country, and if you get easily stressed from having no electricity, you'll need to try and change your perspective a little on life, or buy a generator!

## Corruption

One inevitable topic amongst expats is the corruption in Bali. Indonesia typically ranks at the low end in the Corruption Perception Index; see the transparency.org website for more details. It's a controversial topic, but certainly one that Indonesia is currently struggling with now. All expats have at least one story about having a problem with the police or government official.

While you are required to use an agent for the retirement visa, you can apply for all other visas by yourself. The reality is that this is not always easy and you may need to provide more documentation and visit the immigration office more times yourself than if you use an agent.

An agent will basically hold your hand through the whole experience and you won't even have to visit the immigration office unless you really need to, like when you need to get photographs and fingerprints taken. The agent pays fees to immigration so they can get their job done. Some people might label this as corruption, but this is typically how things work in Indonesia.

People also complain about getting pulled over by the police and having to pay a fine. You often see tourists riding a motorbike without a helmet and sometimes without wearing any shoes or even a shirt! By acting this way, not only is it dangerous, but you only draw attention to yourself from the police. Always look like you know what you are doing, get a local driver's license, be polite, learn to speak a bit of Bahasa Indonesia and you will more than likely never encounter any problems.

## High import duties on alcohol and luxury items

Imported goods like alcohol and food carry high import duties in Indonesia. A bottle of wine can typically cost two or three times more than what you would pay in your home country. Imported cheeses and meats are also quite expensive. For beer drinkers, the local Bintang beer is reasonably cheap, however. Because of the high cost of alcohol in Bali, some locals make a drink from palm sap called *arak*. Sometimes it is laced with methanol and can cause blindness or even death. If you want to try arak, make sure you buy it from a large store or supermarket and avoid cheap home brews that are sometimes sold on the side of the road.

## Walking ATM

In general most people with the means to travel to Bali are better off than most of the local population. There is a perception that foreigners have access to unlimited wealth, and even if you don't have a dollar to your name, most people will think that you are just another rich *bule* (foreigner). Many people will try to take advantage of this by charging you more than what a local would pay for the same product or service. Some people will put up with it and others will send their local friend to go shopping on their behalf. Certainly learning the language and researching prices before making any significant purchases can help get around the 'white skin tax' as some expats call it.

## Property Ownership

Another negative that might affect your decision to retire in Bali is the restriction on foreign ownership of freehold property in Indonesia. You have the option of long term leases and the option of buying property using an Indonesian person's name (nominee), but you cannot buy freehold property in your own name. There is some discussion about changing these laws, but it is unlikely they will change in the near future.

# *The positives*

There are of course many things to like about living in Bali and if you have been to Bali you will probably have your own reasons as to why you want to live there. Different things appeal to different people, but here are some things that I think people enjoy about living in Bali:

## People

One of the most common reasons I have heard from people about why they love Bali is the people. If you visit any tropical island, you will generally find the people to be laid back and easy going and Bali is no exception.

When Balinese have financial and relationship problems, they don't seem to get stressed about these problems like we do in western countries. Balinese are typically warm and friendly and it is pretty rare to see anyone become openly angry.

Some expats warn of getting too taken in by the friendly smile, but I have to agree with a peson who said, "I prefer a fake smile than a sour face."

## Weather

Bali lies just 8 degrees south of the equator, so it's warm all year round, with an average temperature of 31 degrees celsius. It might take some time to get used to the weather for people coming from colder climates. Not only is the weather great for doing any kind of water sports, it also has an effect on the way people live. People tend to sit outside more. In the evenings many people chat with their friends and neighbors, rather than sitting around a television, for example.

The rainy season in Bali runs from around October to April, and you can usually expect a shower of rain every day and the occasional tropical storm.

If you don't like the hot weather or you just want to get away from it occasionally, you can head up to the hills in areas like Bedugul or Munduk, where it's much cooler.

## Cost of living

In general, it should cost you less to live on a day to day basis in Bali. Food, gasoline, staff salaries, etc., are all generally cheaper than what you are probably used to paying and we will explore this more in a separate section.

Activities

For some people who have worked their whole life, retirement can sometimes be a scary thought and it's not unusual to think, "What am I going to do all of the time?" If one partner has been at home, while the other worked, it might be very difficult to adjust with both partners being at home all of the time.

I have met people who were thinking of moving to Bali and they wondered how they would fill in their day. Time in Bali and to Balinese has a very different concept to what most western people will be used to. Life in Bali can be as busy or relaxing as you want. There's so much to do in terms of outdoor physical activities, travel, meeting people, clubs, charities, events and ceremonies. I am pretty sure you will never feel 'bored' living in Bali. Bali has a way of helping you to just stop, relax and take in the scenery and the beauty of the island.

Here are just some of things you could do to occupy your time:

- Surfing
- Golf
- Wind surfing/kite surfing
- Swimming
- Scuba diving/snorkeling
- Travel
- Hiking
- Supporting charities/NGOs
- Joining a club
- Learning Bahasa Indonesia/Balinese
- Cooking classes
- Art classes – painting, silver smith, pottery, batik, wood carving
- Dance
- Yoga
- Balinese music – gamelan, suling (bamboo flute)
- Eating out
- Gardening

- Massage
- Day spas

## Health and well-being

While Bali's hospitals are not the best in the world, Bali can arguably be a fantastic place for preventative medicine. It is certainly something that I'm no expert on, but Bali seems to have an above average number of spas, massage therapists and holistic healing centers, particularly in Ubud.

There are plenty of centers offering services like:

- Meditation
- Reiki
- Yoga
- Healing
- Chakra balancing

While the effectiveness of these treatments is debatable, for people who are into these kinds of treatments Bali is a fantastic place, and most of these centers are very well priced.

## Community life

I had been to Bali a couple of times before I came to live here. The holidays were usually fairly short, just one to two weeks at a time. I enjoyed meeting all of the different people I came across, from tour guides, taxi drivers and guest house owners.

It wasn't until I moved here and was living in a small village that I realized the strong community spirit that's still very alive and well in Bali. I'd been used to living in cities where you could be living next door to someone for years and you might never speak to them, other than the occasional greeting.

Everyone is closely connected to everyone else and there are definitely no secrets in Bali! It can be a great way of living, and the more you can get involved in your community, the more enjoyable your life will be. Of course not everything is rosy all of the time and people have their share of problems and disputes. Everyone you pass, however, will give you a friendly wave and say hello.

An expat who has lived in Bali a long time said to me that even amongst Balinese, the people that are active in their village tend to be healthier and live longer than those that don't like to get involved in community activities.

Safety

Bali is one of the safest places I have been to. I have been robbed once and I lost a computer and some money, but I believe that can happen anywhere in the world. The newspapers carry frequent stories of home break ins, but more often than not, the perpetrators are not from Bali.

Violent crime and muggings are almost unheard of in Bali. It is reasonably safe to walk around at night, you just need to take the usual precautions just as you would anywhere else in the world.

Road safety is a different story, however. Many people drive their cars and motorbikes fairly recklessly and road rules are mostly ignored. If you don't feel comfortable driving, you could always hire a driver. Take extreme care when riding a motorbike, always wear a helmet and make sure to check and see if your insurance covers riding a motorbike or driving in Indonesia.

Many roads and pavements are not well maintained so even if you walk around, you need to be careful of uncovered drains and random holes.

Food

Balinese and Indonesian cuisine might not be as well known as Chinese or Thai, but you can be guaranteed that you will never go hungry. There is a huge selection of local and western style restaurants that are generally well priced and great value. As with all countries in south east Asia, there is a fantastic range of tropical fruits, some of which you may have never seen before.

A certain X-factor

I mentioned earlier that neither Bali or Indonesia usually make it on any top lists for places for retirement so even with the negative points that I have listed, what makes people want to retire in Bali? And if you want to be able to own your own property and live in a country where the government actively promotes programs for foreign retirees, like Malaysia, what is the attraction with Bali?

Everyone is going to have their own reasons for wanting to live in Bali. It's something I have thought about quite a bit. I believe people who have been living in Bali for a few years have a bit of a sense of adventure.

Sure expats love to get together and talk about the problems they've had with their landlords or immigration officials and internet forums and blogs written by expats are full of stories of the 'hardships' foreigners face living in Bali. I think for some people, however, that even though they moan and complain about corruption or problems with visas, deep down they enjoy dealing these kinds of things and it at least creates some interesting stories to tell their friends back home.

Some people love living in Bali and others leave after only a few months. Bali is certainly not going to suit everyone.

## *What if I don't like it?*

Moving overseas and permanently living overseas in any country is a big decision and quite different from taking a short trip. If it's your first time living overseas, rather than just traveling for business or pleasure, there will certainly be a period of adjustment.

There are bound to be people who later find out living in Bali just wasn't for them. I think it is going to take more courage admitting that moving to Bali just wasn't for you and trying a different country, or moving back home, rather than trying to 'stick it out' in Bali and making your own life and the people around you miserable.

It is quite typical for expats to go through certain phases after they have moved overseas. The first period is the honeymoon or holiday phase when everything is great and it's just being like being on a long holiday. The next phase is a period of disappointment which is usually triggered by a negative experience. It is usually after having this negative experience, that you start to question whether you made the right decision to move to Bali. If you make it through this experience, however, you will then enter a period of acceptance when life in your new country starts to take on a sense of normality.

There is probably going to be several times in the beginning when you start wondering if you made the right decision about moving to Bali. It happened to me when I moved to Bali and my house was robbed. I wondered if Bali was safe and started thinking maybe we should move somewhere else, but then I realized home robberies can happen anywhere in the world.

If you start having doubts about your move, think back to the reasons why you wanted to retire in Bali in the first place. I know many people who have troubles in one country, then move to another country and then find they aren't happy there either. There really is no perfect place to live in the world; everywhere is going to have its negative and positive points.

I think it's important to ease as slowly into the move as possible. I know it is not always practical, but I would suggest moving to Bali first for say six months. Rent a furnished house and rent a motorbike or car. This way you can get a good feeling of what it is like living in Bali before you make any large financial decisions, like selling your house in your home country or buying property or a car in Bali.

If you can survive your first major setback, you will then gradually assimilate more into the culture and grow accustomed to doing things differently from your home country, whether it is shopping, cooking or driving a car. You will slowly make more friends with local people and expats and possibly develop new interests. Your life then starts to feel 'normal' again and you start appreciating your new life in Bali. Sure, there will be some things that bother you about living in Bali, but you start to live with those things and perhaps even later, you won't even consider them to be problems.

# Facing your fears

When I surveyed people for this book, one of the concerns that some people had was "fear of the unknown".  If you have lived at the same address for most of your life, in the same country where you were born and move to a completely different country than what you're used to, it's only natural you are going to feel some anxiety.

There are so many things you need to think about like "what if I get sick?", "what about my children?"  I remember getting completely stressed out when I was about to start a new job.  "What if I don't get along with my co-workers?" or "what if I can't do the job?"  In the end, everything eventually worked out.

I believe change is a good thing. I remember reading a book with a fantastic title, "Feel the fear and do it anyway".  I was a little disappointed with the book, but the title has stuck in my mind ever since I heard it and I think it is a good way to live life.

I've seen people on message boards who wrote about moving overseas and then a couple of years later, they posted yet another question about moving. In all of that time, they were still planning and thinking about moving.  I realize that moving to another country is not a light decision, but I think it is better to give something a try and fail, rather than spending your whole life asking yourself, "what if".

## *Part time living in Bali*

If moving lock, stock and barrel to Bali seems a bit daunting, you may want to consider living in Bali just a few months a year.  After my grandparents retired, they rented an apartment on the Gold Coast in Australia for many years, to escape Melbourne's cold winters.  The advantage is that you can keep your house and all of your belongings and still be able to see your friends and family, if that is important to you.

In Bali, you can then just stay in a hotel, or homestay for a few months, without having to bring all of your worldly possessions and have the best of both worlds. Or if you have a property in your home country and in Bali, you could rent out the property when you are away from one of them.

You could also save some money by just using tourist visas or a social visa to come to Bali. If you have another favorite place in the world, you might want to consider dividing your time between two or more different places.

# Preparation and planning

It goes without saying that the more preparation and planning you can do for your retirement and move to Bali, it will help to maintain your levels of stress and ensure that you won't be leaving on the next plane out of Bali. Moving house can be a stressful enough experience, let alone moving to a new country.

Preparation and planning can take on several forms, including both physical and mental. The physical preparation includes moving your possessions, getting visas, organizing your finances and finding accommodation. Then mental side includes examining the reasons why you want to move to Bali. You should also even consider that it might make more sense to keep living in your home country, but just visit Bali for extended holidays.

Another consideration is your health. Only a doctor can really answer this question, it is certainly something you really need to take into account as hospitals and health care in Bali is not the best in the world.

## *When to move*

You might want to consider moving to Bali outside of the high season, when it's less busy and prices for flights and accommodation are less expensive. High season is around July-August and December-January. Another consideration is the weather. Bali only has two seasons, wet and dry. So, it might be preferable to move in the dry season, which starts around April and goes through to September.

# 100 point moving check list

There is a huge amount of planning to be done before moving to Bali. I have created this list of 100 things to do, to help you prepare for the move.

100. Start thinking about if you really want to live in Bali. Think about whether living in Bali is going to be right for you.

99. Make a list of all of the pros and cons of moving to Bali.

98. Set up internet banking in your home country and get an ATM card which can work on one of the global networks like CIRRUS, Maestro or PLUS. As long as you take the necessary precautions internet banking can be very useful way to manage your finances while living overseas. A credit card is also good to have for unexpected emergencies.

97. Start researching properties for rent on the internet. Most properties advertised on the internet are more expensive than finding them yourself while in Bali, but you will need somewhere to stay initially.

96. Get a complete medical checkup before you move to Bali. Check to see if you can purchase any required medication in Bali or if you will need to take it with you.

95. While you are getting checked out, it is probably a good idea to also make an appointment with a dentist. Bali does have some well qualified dentists and expensive treatments can be much cheaper in Bali than your home country. This can also be something worth looking into.

94. Investigate international moving companies if you are planning to move all of your belongings to Bali.

93. If you use an international moving company, make an inventory list of everything you want to take, which you will need for insurance and customs.

92. Think about how you will be accessing your money while in Bali. Like whether you will have money wired to a local bank account or whether you will use an international ATM card.

91. Think about what visa you plan to get and how you plan to go about getting it. See the visa section for more details.

90. Make copies of all of your important documents, like your birth certificate, passport, insurance, driver's license, marriage certificate. You never know if or when you might need these documents and they will definitely be good to have, should you lose anything important.

89. Think about your pets. There are currently strict requirements about bringing animals to Bali because of the problems with rabies and it can be extremely difficult or even impossible to bring dogs or cats to Bali right now.

88. It probably goes without saying, but you should try to read as much as you can about Bali and Indonesia before you come.

87. Do as much research as possible about living in Bali on the internet. The Bali expat forum (balipod.com) and the Indonesia expat forum (www.livinginindonesiaforum.org/) are great places to get up to date information on what it is like to live in Indonesia.

86. There might be a period of time when you move to Bali and when your health insurance starts, so you might need to look into purchasing travel

insurance to cover you for the first few months.

85. Clothes shopping. While Bali has an endless supply of shops selling cheap beach clothing, you might have trouble finding the right size for anything other than t-shirts, especially if you are a larger person. You don't really need formal clothes, but it is nice to have at least a couple sets of clothes for more formal occasions. Wearing flip-flops and board shorts into an immigration office is a definite no-no.

84. Make a list of possessions that you really can't imagine leaving behind.

83. Start marking items in your house that you want to sell, give or throw away. You can buy almost anything these days in Bali, so you don't necessarily have to ship everything.

82. Look into shipping options for what things you can't carry on the plane with you.

81. Prepare to ship items before you arrive and check any electrical appliances or electronic equipment for voltage before shipping.

80. Arrange storage for things which you are planning to leave behind.

79. Sell your car. It really isn't worth the hassle of trying to ship a car to Bali, with all of the required paper work and duties you will need to pay.

78. Start preparing to live in the tropics. For people coming from colder climates, this could take some getting used to.

77. Visit your doctor and get the necessary vaccines and inoculations.

Tetanus, hepatitis, typhus are some vaccines that you want to talk to your doctor about and get booster shots if necessary.

76. Consider what you will do with your house. If you are renting you will need to give notice to your landlord.

75. If you own your own house, you will need to consider selling it or renting it out.

74. Pay back any debts that you owe and try to clear the money you owe on your credit cards.

73. Get a bunch of passport photos before you leave. You will often need them for visa, licenses etc. If possible get them taken with a red background as this seems the favored background color for Indonesia.

72. Research cheap plane tickets and try to organize your depature outside of major holiday periods if you want to save some money.

71. Create or update your will.

70. Make an appointment with your financial advisor and make sure you get your finances in order before you leave.

69. Make a budget. Living in Bali can be cheap, but it can be easy to spend a lot of money on going out and fancy dinners if you are not too careful. Research possible places you would like to live in Bali.

68. Consider joining Viber (http://www.viber.com/) which allows you to make free local and international telephone calls using Wifi internet.

67. Start to learn Bahasa Indonesia. It is not too difficult to pick up and it will really make life in Bali so much more enjoyable. Learning Indonesian (www.learningindonesian.com) is a fantastic site with free downloadable lessons.

66. If you have kids, research schools which you might like to send them to.

65. Speak to your family and friends about your move.

64. Make sure your spouse is just as eager as you about the move.

63. If you have elderly parents, think about who is going to take care of them. What is going to happen to them if they get sick?

62. Think about exactly when you want to move. If you are currently working, give yourself some time off between when you retire and when you move.

61. Try to make a couple of visits before you decide to move to Bali on a permanent basis. Travel around the island so you can become familiar with the different parts.

60. Get your international driver's license. It might take some time before you get your visa sorted out and be able to get a local one.

59. Research community groups that you might want to join in Bali, like Rotary. Joining a club like Rotary will help you to make friends and build a support network.

58. Learn to bargain when shopping. Don't be afraid to ask for a discount.

57. Learn how to ride a motor bike. Motor bikes are a great way to get around the island.

56. Create a "to do" list for once you arrive in Bali

55. Travel to other parts of Indonesia.

54. Get used to having less privacy in Bali.

53. Research foundations and charities that you might consider supporting in Bali.

52. Start learning to be a patient person. If you don't like sitting in line, get into the habit of taking a book or an iPod when you go to somewhere like a bank.

51. Consider buying an ebook reader like a Kindle. Books are heavy and the selection is not so large in book shops in Bali.

50. Consider buying a laptop computer. The newer netbooks are compact and very portable.

49. Fill up on your favorite foods before you go: You may not have them again for a while (Though you will find new favorites).

48. When buying tickets, consider a layover for a couple of days to get

used to the time change / see new things.

47. Consider buying some small souvenirs from your home country to give as gifts for people.

46. Have dinner in an Indonesian restaurant if your city has one so you can get used to the food.

45. Start learning to cook Asian style dishes. Except for expensive western style villas, most houses don't have ovens. Most cooking is done on a gas stove. Cooking Asian style dishes will also help to save money.

44. Get a small amount of rupiah at your bank so you don't have to change money at the airport and you can catch a taxi to your accommodation.

43. Call your bank and tell them you are traveling to Indonesia, so they won't flag your credit or debit cards.

42. Check when your passport will expire. For the retirement visa you need to have more than 18 months remaining. Also traveling in and out of Indonesia and getting various visas and extensions, you fill up your passport pretty quick, so you might want to consider getting a new passport if you don't have many pages left. It is going to be easier to get in your home country than after you arrive in Bali.

41. Once you have booked your flight, check how much luggage you can bring on the plane. Airlines are pretty strict on this now and excess luggage can get very expensive.

40. Cancel or redirect any newspaper or magazine subscriptions you might get delivered.

39. Decide how you want to receive your mail. It could be sometime before you get a mailing address in Bali, so it might be a good idea to ask a friend or relative if you can get mail delivered to their address. You could look into using a mail forwarding service.

38. If you know roughly where you will be living in Bali, consider getting a PO box. They are pretty cheap and you don't need any special visa to get one.

37. Check when your driver's license will expire. It will be easier to get it renewed when you are in your home country than when you move overseas.

36. Meet your accountant and find out about your tax situation while living overseas.

35. Pay a visit to any friends or relatives you haven't seen in a while.

34. Set up a Skype account. It is a great way to stay in touch with family and friends. Make sure they are also familiar with it.

33. If you wear glasses, consider buying a new pair while you are at home.

32. Set up another bank account with ATM card so at least you have another account with a different bank in case the first one doesn't work for any reason.

31. It probably goes without saying, but don't touch any form of drugs while you are in Indonesia or consider bringing them in your case.

30. Get your existing phone "unlocked" so you can use a local SIM card when you arrive in Bali. Most people use prepaid SIM cards, rather than having a monthly plan. Consider getting a basic $20-$30 mobile as expensive phones can go missing pretty quickly.

29. If you have been neglecting your health, now is a good time to get in shape again.

28. Consider learning a new hobby that you can take up in Bali, like yoga, surfing or scuba diving.

27. Start to get used to eating spicy food.

26. Be prepared for some ups and downs. Living in Bali isn't all plain sailing.

25. If you are coming to Bali as a single man or woman be very careful about falling in love with the wrong person. Many people have lost substantial amounts of money from being scammed by a lover.

24. If you want to start a business consider buying "How to start a business in Bali". Just remember though, that you have no rights to work on a retirement visa.

23. Return any library books that are overdue.

22. Have a garage sale of all of the things you won't be taking to Bali.

21. Find out where your country's embassy is in Indonesia and whether

they have a consulate in Bali. This kind of information is useful to know.

20. Sign up to Facebook if haven't done so already. It is a great way to keep in touch with old and new friends and family.

19. With the high cost of alcohol in Indonesia, consider learning to make your own wine or beer - just don't try and sell it!

18. Sign up for a free email address such as Gmail. With Gmail you never have to delete old messages and the search function is very powerful.

17. Research insurance plans and make sure they include emergency evacuation.

16. Check if your insurance includes coverage if you ride a motorbike.

15. Research the local hospital and health care options available in Bali.

14. Spend time reading about the history of Indonesia and Bali, the different religions and ethnic groups.

13. If you really must buy a house, consider what options you have for ownership.

12. Consider contacting a Bali based charity or orphanage to see if they need help transporting anything to Bali.

11. If you are coming from a country with high speed internet, start to get used to life with very slow internet, emphasis on slow!

10. Start looking into what internet options are available in the area you are planning to live in Bali.

9. Leave your furniture at home. You can buy some fantastic furniture in Bali and custom made stuff is relatively cheap.

8. Consider buying an external hard drive and copying all of your photos and old movies to it.

7. Plan your going away party.

6. Organize your transport to the airport.

5. Research the culture.

4. Research the culture..

3. Research the culture….

2. Make a goal and stick with it. Give that goal enough time to succeed on its own merits.

1. Remember why you are leaving. Make certain your expectations are realistic.

# Adapting to the culture

One of the biggest mistakes expats make when moving to a foreign country like Indonesia is trying to recreate their home and lifestyle that they are used to from back home.  On one hand you don't want to ditch everything you're used to, but on the other hand you need to open your mind up to a different culture, a different way of thinking and a different way of doing things in general.  Perhaps some people will see moving to Bali as though they are just moving house; packing up their belongings and moving to a different country, as though they were moving to a new neighborhood.

In many ways when you move to Bali you may find yourself learning to live again.  For people who embrace the change this can only be a positive step.  For people who constantly compare everything to the way things are "done at home" they may find themselves on the next plane out not soon after they arrive.  If you come to live in Bali knowing that you will have to learn new things and accept this as a new challenge in your life, you will likely have a much more favorable experience.

I have lived most of my life in Asia and I found that many people who go to a foreign country for long periods of time usually fall into three groups.  The first group are people who have usually been sent overseas on a work assignment for their company or have gone overseas solely for the purpose of making money.  This type of person will live in company supplied housing and spend most of their time working.  They don't have the time to learn a new language and they usually  only associate with people from their office and with other expats.

They may also have left family and partners at home.  This group of people is usually very miserable as they usually have no interest in the country they are living in.  They are there for work only.  They have a lot of difficulty dealing with the local people and they try to live their lives as though they were in their own country.

On the other extreme you have people who go totally native.  They become fluent in the local language, eat only local food and only hang out with local people.  They shun everything and sometimes everyone from their home country and living a 'western' lifestyle.

Both of these cases are the extreme and the people who seemed to me the happiest, are the expats who find balance between the two extremes, the people who learn the local language and have local friends, but also have a group of expat friends from their own country or another foreign country. Many local people will be interested in learning about your country and they will also appreciate the efforts you make to speak their language and learn about their culture.

Some people think that they have to go totally native to try and fit in more. I don't think that this is necessarily the case. Of course the more of the language you know, the easier life will be, but I don't think you have to do everything as a local would to get accepted by people.

I lived in Japan for 10 years and I don't want to say Balinese culture is anything like Japan, but I did see many expats wrestle with these types of issues, including myself. It took me a long time to realize it, but in the end I came to the conclusion that you just need to be yourself. Locals know that you are not one of them, so I don't think it is worth trying to act like them.

They will be used to the way foreigners act and will be half expecting that you don't know how to act exactly how they do. Having said that, it is extremely important to have the utmost respect for the country you are living in. It is still important to study and try to understand the culture. If you visit a temple for example, you should follow the expected rules, like dressing appropriately.

By saying that you should act how you normally act, if you are a loud and obnoxious drunk, you might want to change your behavior pretty quick, or please stay at home! Like everything in life, there is a time and place for everything.

I am pretty sure you will have a much more enjoyable time in Bali if you try to make real friendships with local people and include them into your lives. As I wrote before, it is all about trying to create a good balance.

# Language

English is widely spoken in Bali and you can get by fairly comfortably in the main tourist areas. I would strongly suggest, however, that you make every effort to learn Bahasa Indonesia - Indonesia's national language. Almost every ethnic group has its own language and Bahasa Indonesia is the common language spoken by most Indonesians across the archipelago.

Not only will it be easier to communicate with local people, but it will help to open up new doors to your life in Bali. You will earn a fair amount of respect from the locals by being able to speak the language and it shows to them that you have a strong interest in their country and culture. It can even save you money when you can bargain in the local language. Bali also has its own language and it is good to learn a few words of this also, but you should try to become comfortable with Bahasa Indonesia first.

Bahasa Indonesia is a comparatively easy language to learn. It is written in roman characters, so you will immediately start to remember words just from looking at the various signs, like "Apotek" for chemist or pharmacy. To go from knowing a few words and phrases to being able to make a conversation does require some effort to study. From my own experience studying languages I would say you really just need to concentrate on doing a little bit every day, rather than trying to cram all of your study into just a few days. You will start recognizing words that you hear and be able to answer basic questions that people will ask every day, like, "Where are you from?" and "What is your name?"

If you have already made the decision to move to Bali, I would recommend doing a short study course in Indonesian at a college before you arrive. There are many good language guides that you should be able to find at any good book store or online through Amazon. I recommend the Learning Indonesian (www.learningindonesian.com) online course. They have free and paid lessons and study guides that you can download. Their lessons are available in MP3 audio format, so you can download them to your favorite MP3 player and listen to them while you are out walking or driving the car.

Once you are in Bali it is a good idea to get a language teacher. Try and find someone who has experience teaching languages.

For actual places to study, you could try the Starfish Language Center in Ubud, which is a non-profit organization (www.starfishubud.com) that teaches Balinese children and adults languages to help with their job prospects and charges a small fee for expats to learn Indonesian. Also in Ubud is Cinta Bahasa (www.cintabahasa.com), another place which gets good reviews from expats.

In Denpasar you can try IALF, an Australian run program (www.ialf.edu)

The most important thing is to make a start and perservere with it. It's very easy to get a little lazy when you're in Bali and the time passes by fairly quickly. I guarantee, however, that you will have a far more rewarding experience in Bali by being able to speak the language.

# Relationships

Whether you are moving to Bali as a couple or you are single, developing friendships and relationships with local Balinese will definitely make your stay more enjoyable. Many people from all over Indonesia come to find work in Bali, so you can also meet locals from all over Indonesia.

As long as you come across as a decent person, you will find Balinese to be very welcoming and supportive. Some cynical people would say that locals only do this for some kind of monetary gain, and while some people may have this motivation, you tend to quickly find out who is genuine and who is not.

If you are single, whether you are male or female, you will suddenly find yourself receiving a great deal more attention than what you might be accustomed to. Stories abound of foreigners buying their new partner a motorbike, only to disappear when they get the keys in their hand.

I also know a foreigner who put his property solely in the name of his girlfriend and much of his savings in a local bank in her name as well. He has since had to go back to his home country for medical treatment and the last I heard he was living in a hotel in his home country because he had sold his house there and he was no longer on good terms with his family.

On the other hand I know of many mixed couples in healthy relationships, despite a large age difference and obvious language and cultural differences. While it might be a lot of fun dating someone young and attractive, it is certainly not without its complications. HIV awareness is quite low in Bali, despite reports of growing rates of infection. Tread softly —particularly when you first arrive.

# Banking and finance

One of the benefits of getting a retired visa is being able to open a bank account in your own name. A KITAS is required to open a bank account in Indonesia. Although, you sometimes hear about banks who are prepared to bend the rules and allow foreigners to open an account without a KITAS.

It's possible to live in Bali without a local bank account and to just use your bank account from home with an attached ATM card. This is fine for day to day living, but you could run into problems if you need to purchase a large ticket item like a house or car. Most banks will charge an even higher transaction fee for withdrawals made overseas. Shop around as you might be able to find a bank in your home country that doesn't charge for withdrawals made overseas.

You could save on ATM fees also by having your own local bank account as the fees on withdrawing your money from a local bank account are significantly less than withdrawing money from an overseas account. There is of course a fee with wiring your money to Indonesia, but as long as you do just a few large amounts, it could be much less in the long run, than relying on making many withdrawals from an overseas account.

One of the biggest financial concerns retirees face is inflation. If you live in a foreign country, but your income or your pension comes from another country, you will have the added problem with foreign currency fluctuations. If your income is in US dollars for example, you would have experienced a loss in purchasing power of the past couple of years, as the rupiah has been on the increase and the US dollar's value has significantly fallen.

Some banks allow you to have multiple currency accounts. By having such an account, you can transfer your money to Indonesia without being affected by the exchange rate and then change it to rupiah when the rate is more favorable.

## Opening a bank account

Along with the many Indonesian banks, there are a few foreign banks starting to open up in Bali. If the bank you use has a branch in Bali, there could be advantages of opening an account in Bali with the same bank.

The most prominent foreign bank in Bali is the Commonwealth Bank from Australia. You will still, however, be required to do an international transfer if you want to transfer money from your home bank account to your account in Indonesia as the banks in Australia and Indonesia are still separate entities.

There are several large banks in Indonesia all offering similar standards of service. The state owned banks include: Bank Negara Indonesia (BNI), Bank Rakyat Indonesia (BRI) and Bank Mandiri. Some of the foreign exchange banks include, CIMB Niaga, BCA, Danamon and Permata.

While banks may have some people who speak English, it might be a good idea to take an Indonesian friend along to open your account, if you don't speak Indonesian. Don't forget to take your passport and your immigration blue book, which you receive from immigration after getting your retirement visa.

## Changing Money

Since Bali gets so many foreign tourists, there are money changers everywhere. Some money changers, however, offer rates that are above the market rate. When the rate is too good to be true, there is usually some kind of scam involved. Some of the scams include fake notes, faulty calculators and money disappearing while it is being counted. Count the money out yourself and never let the money changer touch your cash again after you have counted it. Shops and markets that have a money changer working out the back, are some of the worst offenders.

While banks may not offer the best rates, at least you know there is less likelihood of being cheated and highly recommended if you are changing a large amount of money. Going to a money changer that gives you a proper receipt, is also a good idea. Many places also only accept, or give a better rate for newer US dollar bills, that aren't worn.

## Credit Cards

A credit card is useful to have while traveling and living overseas. It's useful to have in an emergency and for paying for things online such as airline tickets. If you already have one from your own country, you could just use that. If it expires while you are living overseas you will need to get a new one sent to you in Bali. If it is about to expire before you leave for Bali, it could be a good idea to organize a new one, before your departure. Due to high levels of credit card fraud in Indonesia, an Indonesian credit card may not work for purchases outside of the country.

## Australian Aged Pension

It is possible to live overseas and still claim the Australian aged pension if you meet all of the requirements, ie. Income and assets test.

If you have any questions about getting the Australian aged pension it is a good idea to speak to the international division of Centrelink who are located in Hobart. Their number is: +61 3 6222 3455.

## LPD Savings Banks

Bali has many LPD savings banks, which are small saving and lending institutions for the local community. Money is typically lent out at high interest rates, and it is possible to get high rates of return on fixed deposits. Foreigners are welcome to deposit money and you may not even need to have a KITAS depending on the bank. Each bank is closely linked to a village. The banks, however, are not regulated by the central bank of Indonesia. If people hear that a certain bank is having a problem, people may rush to withdraw their money, and while the high returns might appear atrractive, it's obviously not a good idea to put all of your money in one LPD.

# Shopping

Whether you are renting or moving into a new house, you will need to spend sometime shopping for household goods after you move to Bali. In my opinion, it is easier and possibly cheaper, selling all of your possessions and then buying new furniture and electronic goods when you move to Bali. Electronic goods, furniture and general household goods are reasonably priced.

## *Food and household goods*

A good place to start is Lotte Mart (www.lottemart.co.id) in Sanur (formerly Makro). It is intended for bulk purchasing for restaurants and hotels, but it is also open to the general public. You can get a discount card, if you spend over a certain amount, and they send you catalogues in the mail. They have a reasonable selection of white goods, kitchen supplies, household goods and a wide range of food that you would find in any supermarket.

The other main supermarkets are Carrefour and Hypermart. Both sell food, household goods, furniture and electronic goods like televisions and white goods. Hardys is a Balinese owned supermarket chain with stores in several of the major tourist centers in Bali. It is hard to say which store is the cheapest. Range and prices vary from store to store and you will eventually find your preferred grocery store for shopping. Bali Deli (www.balideli.net) in Seminyak is one of the best gourmet and imported food stores in Bali. There is an Australian butcher (Raja Meats) located in Jalan Danau Posor, Sanur.

## *Computers*

The best place in Bali to stock up on computer supplies is the REMO store in Denpasar, located on Jalan Dipnegoro opposite the Ramayana store.

Spread over several floors, it is made up of many small stores selling computers, laptops, phones and other electronic items like security systems. Many shops also do computer repair. There is an authorized Apple reseller in the Carrefour store on Sunset Road.

## Shopping Malls

Bali Galeria located near the Simpang Siur roundabout, is one of the largest malls in Bali and has the greatest range of shops under the one roof, including ACE Hardware and Hypermart Supermarket. In the front building, there is a duty free shopping mall, featuring a number of international brand shops, with high prices quoted in US dollars. The mall is located behind this building. The mall also has several places for eating and central courtyard with outdoor seating areas.

The other large shopping mall is Istana Kuta Galeria. It is targeted mainly to tourists and is located right on the beach. On the top floor, there is an electronics store and hardware store selling a range of household goods.

## Books

Periplus (periplus.co.id) is the largest English language book store chain in Bali. They have stores in all of the large malls and tourist centers in Bali. The range is not so great, however, but you can usually find latest best selling paperbacks and travel guides. For second hand books, Ganesha (www.ganeshabooksbali.com) in Ubud (opposite the post office), has a good selection of new and second hand books. They also offer a refund when you return the book. With the large number of expats living in Ubud, there is always a fresh supply of books.

## Furniture

There are many large and small furniture manufacturers in Bali and a significant amount gets exported overseas. Prices are reasonable for custom made furniture, but you do need to bargain. Here are just a couple of the more well known stores:

**Bali ERom Furniture**

Jl. Raya Kerobokan No. 124 Kuta
62-361-733241
http://www.balieromfurniture.com

**Cempaka Bali**
Jl. Bypass Ngurah Rai 8, Simpang Siur, Kuta
0361 747 4393
http://www.cempaka.biz/

**Christy Furniture**
Jl. Raya Kerobokan No. 98
Banjar Taman, Kuta
62.361.735502
http://www.christy-furniture.com/

# Hospitals and medical care

Hospitals and medical care is one area that could be a concern for people thinking of retiring in Bali. Certainly, there has been some improvement with the growth of tourism, but for serious illnesses most expats tend to fly to Singapore, Australia or Malaysia. Medical evacuation is not cheap and could send you bankrupt without insurance, so make sure your policy covers this.

## *Hospitals in Bali*

The main hospitals frequented by foreigners in Bali include: Denpasar General Hospital (RSUP Sanglah), Prima Medika Hospital, BIMC Hospital, Surya Husada Hospital, Bali Med Hospital and Kasih Ibu Hospital. Sanglah is the largest public hospital in Bali. Prima Medika Hospital, BIMC Hospital, Surya Husada Hospital, Bali Med Hospital and Kasih Ibu Hospital are private hospitals.

**Sanglah Public Hospital**
Jl. Kesehatan Selatan 1
Sanglah Denpasar

Tel: +62 361 227 911 - 15
Fax: +62 361 226 363

**Prima Medika Hospital**
Jl. P Serangan 9x, Denpasar
Tel: +62 361 236225

**Kasih Ibu Hospital**
Jl. Teuku Umar 120 Denpasar
Tel: (+62 361) 223 036
Fax: (+62 361) 268 690

**BIMC Hospital**
Jl. Bypass Ngurah Rai No. 100X
Kuta 80361
Tel: +62-361 761 263

Fax: +62-361 764 345
E-mail: info@bimcbali.com
website: www.bimcbali.com


**Surya Husada Hospital**
Jl. P. Serangan 1
Denpasar
Tel: +62-361 233787 or 235041
Fax: +62 361 231177


**Bali Med Hospital**
Jl Mahendradatta no 57X
Denpasar
Tel: (+62-361) 484748
Fax: (+62-361) 484748


**International SOS**
Jl. Bypass Ngurah Rai No. 505X
Kuta 80361
Tel: +62-361 710 505
Fax: +62-361 710 515
E-mail: baliassistoperation@internationalsos.com
Website: www.sos-bali.com


The following are two interviews I did with International SOS and BIMC Hospital. They are two of the leading hospitals in Bali providing health care to expatriates. They provided some useful information on medical care for people planning on retiring in Bali.

# Interview with International SOS Hospital

*1. Is there anything people can do to prepare for their stay in Bali to prevent medical problems later?*

If you have any medical conditions, you need to check beforehand whether medications or treatment are available in Bali. You also need to check if your vaccinations are up to date.

*2. Are there any injections or inoculations people should get before they come to Bali?*

Tetanus booster, pre-exposure rabies, Typhoid, Hepatitis A and B vaccinations.

*3. What are some of the common illnesses older foreigners might face in Bali? What measures can they take to prepare for them?*

One of the most common problem arises from slips/trips/falls—therefore fractures. Check your accommodation to ensure tiles are not slippery, particularly in the bathrooms, handrails on steps and appropriate height and width of steps. Being aware of mosquito control, to reduce the chance of dengue fever. Seek medical advice if you are unwell with diarrhea and vomiting; you can become dehydrated more quickly in Bali and this can effect older people more severely and can cause people to appear confused and therefore more at risk of falls.

*4. Are there any kinds of diseases or illnesses that cannot be taken care of in Bali and would require medical evacuation?*

Cancer treatment and palliative care—while cancer treatment is available, the support services and ancillary services are not available. Terminal care for any disease is better handled in your home country. Surgery, particularly for fractures, is better handled outside Bali, particularly for follow up and infection control issues. Rehabilitation is not a well established specialty in Bali and older people will need a good program to ensure they make a full recovery.

**5. Can you give any advice on what kind of medical insurance people should take out?**

You need insurance that covers evacuation from Bali, not only for emergencies, but also if a second opinion is needed from a center of medical excellence, such as Singapore.

**6. What medication is available in Bali? What kinds of medication do people need to bring from overseas?**

It is best to check on a case by case basis. Most common medications are available, not all though. You need to ensure your medication is bought from a reputable source. If you are on regular medication, you can email us directly, prior to coming to Bali and we will check the availability and cost for the medicine.

**7. What advice can you give to people who are coming to live in the tropics for the first time?**

You need to adjusti to the warm weather and humidity; choose what you eat wisely and bring enough supply of your regular medication to allow you time to find a local supply.

**8. Can you provide any tips for staying healthy in Bali, especially for retired people?**

Exercise regularly and get regular medical check ups or regular blood tests if you have any chronic illnesses. Ensure you lead a healthy lifestyle including exercise and a good diet.

**More about International SOS**

International SOS provides primary health care services in Indonesia by operating three clinics of international standards located in Jakarta (Cipete and Kuningan) and Bali, under the name SOS Medika Clinics. Opened in 1985, our clinics are run by a highly trained team of specialized medical and allied health professionals to ensure delivery of superior quality and comprehensive medical care in Indonesia.

International SOS aims to provide our members and visitors with peace of mind by taking care of all health care needs, from primary medical needs to any unforeseen emergencies. Our professional team of doctors, nurses, and clinic staff can provide medical care through our commitment to customer care and implementation of international standards in healthcare services and infection/disease control.

SOS Medika - Bali (Clinic and Alarm Center)
Jl. By Pass Ngurah Rai 505X, Kuta 80221
Clinic Tel. (+62-361) 720 100
Fax: (+62 361) 710 515
24 Hour Alarm Center Tel. 0361 710 505
Email: sos.bali@internationalsos.com
Website www.internationalsos.com
CMO: Dr Susan PRANATA

## *Interview with BIMC Hospital*

*1. Is there anything people can do to prepare for their stay in Bali to prevent medical problems later?*

Vaccination is one method we can use to prevent communicable illness. If you have a medical condition and are on long term medication, we recommend you travel with your medication list on hand. We also recommend that before planning a trip for any period of time, you consult your general practitioner or travel medicine clinic to be sure your vaccinations are current and you are fit to travel.

We strongly recommend that if you plan to travel for a long period of time, you need to confirm whether your destination has your medication available, especially in developing countries such as Indonesia. Some medications are not available in Indonesia. It is also wise to find out whether there are any particular hazards to your personal safety and security at your intended destination, so you can take appropriate precautions. Your embassy can give you further information on any safety and security precautions you should be aware of.

Everyone is advised to have an annual comprehensive health checkup. This comprehensive examination will be an important factor for early detection of a specific disease, or as a baseline examination for further checkups. A healthy lifestyle, such as a good diet, regular exercise, not smoking and avoiding stresses will also help you.

### 2. Are there any injections or inoculations people should get before they come to Bali?

BIMC Hospital adheres to international protocols such as the World Health Organization (WHO) and Centers of Disease Control (CDC). Ensure your vaccinations are current and it is wise to get the recommended vaccines prior travelling to Bali. Currently, the vaccines recommended for travelers to Bali are: Hepatitis A and B, Typhoid and Rabies. Japanese encephalitis is recommended for those who plan to visit or stay in a rural farming area. However, if you have missed any of these vaccinations, most vaccinations are available at BIMC Hospital. BIMC Hospital has an extensive vaccination program for adults and children.

### 3. What are some of the common illnesses older foreigners might face in Bali? What measures can they take to prepare for them?

Some of the more common infections we encounter with the elderly at BIMC Hospital include: Respiratory Tract Infections, Urinary Tract Infections, Gastrointestinal Tract Infections such as diarrhea or typhoid fever etc. Infectious diseases can be prevented by living a healthy life-style which includes drinking plenty of water as well as performing good hygiene and sanitation. Vaccination is another way to prevent from some infectious diseases (Flu vaccine, Typhoid vaccine, Hepatitis etc).

Other common illnesses found in the elderly include: diabetes, heart and kidney problems. The idea is to prevent the condition from getting worse by checking your medical condition regularly with your general practitioner or specialist. This is to ensure your medical condition is controlled well. Regular doctor visits can assist your medical condition as well as following a healthy lifestyle, enjoying a good balanced diet, drinking plenty of water, exercise regularly, enough rest, not smoking and avoiding a stressful lifestyle.

**4. Is there any kind of diseases or illnesses that cannot be taken care of in Bali and would require medical evacuation?**

Most of medical problems can be safely treated in Bali; however, for more complicated cases, for diagnostic purposes or patient preference; there may be a need to evacuate to a higher care facility. Basically, all medical conditions need to be stabilized in Bali before evacuation. BIMC Hospital has developed a select team of medical staff that forms the critical care team including overseeing the management of the medical evacuation. One example that may require a medical evacuation is a heart rhythm disturbance (Arrhythmia) that requires a pacemaker; or heart attack that requires open heart surgery.

**5. Can you give any advice on what kind of medical insurance people should take out?**

We recommend all foreigners take out a comprehensive health insurance including medical evacuation for the destination. Medical costs can be very expensive and/or not readily available. Your health insurance policy should include coverage for emergency repatriation for medical conditions where services are not adequate in the country you are residing, hospitalization, medical care for accident/illness and repatriation of mortal remains.

**6. What medication is available in Bali? What kinds of medication do people need to bring from overseas?**

Most medications are available in Bali; however, sometimes more specific medications need to be ordered in advance from the larger cities such as Jakarta or Surabaya. Sometimes specific medications are not available in the country; therefore we strongly recommend you check the availability of your regular medications prior to travelling to Bali.

**7. What advice can you give to people who are coming to live in the tropics for the first time?**

Besides being familiar with the climate, tropical countries are unique for their humidity. This can be a cause of concern and can give you some medical problems, such as skin problem, fungal infections etc. Infectious diseases are one of the most common problems in the tropics. Another common ailment we see at BIMC is people suffering from dehydration. We recommend you drink plenty of water daily, carry out good hygiene and sanitation and live a healthy lifestyle to reduce your risk.

## 8. Can you provide any tips for staying healthy in Bali, especially for retired people?

A healthy lifestyle is recommended to prevent illnesses such as a heart attack, diabetes, high blood pressure and communicable illnesses such as a lung infection, diarrhea etc. In tropical countries, there are a number of diseases which are transmitted by insects, others are water borne or may be carried by foods, often in meat. There are a number of simple precautions you can take to reduce your risk. To reduce your risk of being bitten by mosquitoes, follow these simple steps: make sure there is no water lying dormant around your house or villa, use insect repellant containing DEET especially at dusk and dawn when mosquitoes are most prevalent, wear long sleeved trousers and shirts, sleep in screened areas, and burn citronella based candles. To avoid infection and disease simply practice good hygiene and sanitation to help reduce your risk.

## 9. Can you please tell me a little bit about your hospital and the treatments you can provide?

BIMC Hospital Kuta is a medical centre which also specializes in Accident and Emergency care. We have developed a select team of medical professionals that form the critical care team. Our hospital is open and ready to assist 24 hours a day.

Services within the hospital include: Accident and Emergency Centre, Medical Centre, Operating Theatre, Hospital beds, Radiology Department with Digital CT Scan, Ultrasound and X-Ray, Pathology Department, Pharmacy, Isolation Rooms, Fully Equipped Ambulances, First Response Emergency Motorbike and medical evacuations.

BIMC Hospital is growing and will open a new hospital in Nusa Dua late 2011. We will expand on the current medical services offered by BIMC Hospital, Kuta by adding new specialty care areas such as a Dialysis Centre, Cosmetic Centre and Dental Services. BIMC Hospital Nusa Dua will serve the surrounding areas of Nusa Dua, Tanjung Benoa, Jimbaran and Uluwatu.

# Health Insurance

Finding good and affordable health insurance is one of the most important things you will need to research before coming to Bali. Some of the things which you will need to take into account, include any pre-existing conditions and your age. Perhaps the main decision you will have to make is whether you take our insurance in your own country, that will cover you overseas or whether to purchase it in Bali.

There are also agents in Bali who sell international health insurance policies, such as BUPA, IMG and William Russell. This is the best kind of policy to get, as it will, or should cover you for any travel you do, emergency medical evacuations and treatment in the overseas country you are evacuated to.

BIMC Bali (www.bimcbali.com), is a hospital which services locals, tourists and expats, has a membership plan which covers GP visits, but does not include things like tests, X-Rays and hospital stays. They do have medical evacuation insurance for a reasonably low fee.

If you are only planning on coming to Bali for a few months at a time, you might be able to just use ordinary travel insurance. Some credit cards even provide travel insurance, which is something you could look into.

For serious injuries and medical care, such as a traffic accident, most hospitals will not be able to provide the treatment necessary, especially in life threatening situations. In these instances, emergency medical evacuation to a nearby country such as Australia or Singapore is necessary. The cost is astronomical and if your insurance doesn't cover you for it, it could send you and your family bankrupt.

Insurance companies are good at taking your money, but you only really find out how good they are until you get sick or injured and you need to make a claim. I have heard of people having an Indonesian driving license but they don't hold a motorbike license in their own country so the insurance company refused to pay. An international driver's license might make it legal for you to drive in Bali, but you might not be covered by your insurance company. The important point is to read the fine print in your policy and try to get in writing the things you are and aren't covered for. Unfortunately, insurance companies love keeping things vague as possible!

I did two interviews with insurance agents to help you to understand how the health insurance companies operate here.

## *Bali Medical Insurance*

### *Please tell us a little bit about your company?*

Bali Medical Insurance has been operating in the region (based here in Bali) for over 12 years. We are specialist providers of International Medical Insurance specifically designed for the expatriate. We are a western owned and run professional company that offers a personalized friendly contact. Although internatimonal edical insurance is our main area of expertise, we also offer travel insurance (both incoming and outgoing) local staff medical coverage, villa/house building and contents coverage and car insurance.

### *Which insurance companies do you represent?*

We provide quotations for those health insurance companies that have a good standing, professional outlook and proven track record only. We are authorized intermediaries for:

  a.  William Russell Elite global insurance plans
  b.  International Medical Group (IMG) plans including Global Select and Global Fusion plans (UK) and Global Medical Insurance (USA) plans.
  c.  Aetna International Health care plans (formerly Goodhealth).
  d.  DKV (Munich) health plans.

### *How should people decide which company to use?*

We help the client to choose the best insurance company and level of cover based on their individual needs and budget.

*What advice can you give to people looking to retire in Bali in deciding what kind of insurance cover they should use?*

We have found that many retirees moving to the region believe they have sufficient cover from previous plans or they have sufficient funds put aside to cover any emergency. When this is the case, we always ask them to check their current policy to be sure their insurance does cover this region and evacuation is included. With bank funds being available I tell them that the cost of a basic evacuation will run over $30.000 (USD) per evacuation and this will not include the cost of treatment etc at the hospital or other incidental costs, whereas the cost of insurance is minimal in comparison.

*Is it possible for people just to use travel insurance and what are the potential problems of doing this?*

Although travel insurance is acceptable for a short stay, it is not recommended for any long term period. This is due to the small limits on benefits available and some cases the client has to pay up front first then claim back, this can be a huge amount if you are looking at evacuation costs to the nearest centre of excellence.

*Should people organize their health insurance before or after they arrive in Bali?*

Moving into a new house and country can be a very stressful time and everything is new and confusing. For this reason I would advise all clients to have insurance coverage organized before they arrive in Bali. Murphy's Law dictates that you will need health insurance if you don't have it.

*What if a person has pre-existing medical conditions?*

Pre-existing conditions are always a grey area and it depends on the individual insurance company. Most insurance will cover you from the date of your plan but previous medical condition will not be covered. However some companies will, if accepted, allow cover for certain medical conditions after a 24 month "moratorium period", as long as these conditions have been advised, they have to go through an underwriter's process for consideration. The client may have to provide medical documentation to support the condition. Some pre existing conditions may be covered by paying a loading, however it still falls to the underwriter's decision.

### How does a person's age affect getting health insurance in Bali?

Health insurance premiums are based on age; the older you are the more expensive it becomes. Most ages are grouped into 4 year bands (i.e. 40-44 years) for pricing purposes. Some companies also have a limit on the age for new clients joining their plans; generally this is around the 65th birthday. Their plan will continue to cover them after this age but new clients must be no older than that.

### How can people make sure they are covered in motorbike or traffic accidents?

Within this region we have made sure that the companies and plans that we offer have adequate accident/ illness covered as an integral part of the plan. So no matter if a traffic accident / a heart attack or general illness, the client is fully covered, even on the basic level plan.

### How important is it to get emergency medical evacuation?

We cannot stress the importance of having medical emergency evacuation enough, if living in a developing country such as Indonesia. It is unfortunate that this region, although having well equipped hospitals with great facilities, it is lacking in medical training and experience with many major medical emergencies. Even minor conditions that normally are treatable can become major problems if treated in Bali. You should also be aware that airlines will not allow you to travel on their planes to seek further treatment elsewhere if you have a medical condition that exceeds their "normal" standards, thereby necessitating the added cost of an evacuation.

### Can you offer any other tips or advice for people thinking of retiring in Bali?

We would advise all expatriate residents to have at least the basic health insurance cover, even just for in hospital coverage (with the added benefit of evacuation) this will offset the huge cost of uninsured medical treatment and evacuation.

The contact details for Bali Medical Insurance are:

Jl Bypass Ngurah Rai 151b Sanur Bali
Office Hrs: 9 am – 5 pm Monday – Friday
Office Ph: 0361 282242
Office fax: 0361 282387
My Hp: 081 2385 8342
Emails: (office) info@balimedicalinsurance.com
Laurie Simons: marketing@balimedicalinsurance.com
Sue Speak: suespeak@balimedicalinsureance.com
Web: www.balimedicalinsurance.com

## BH Financial Services

*Please tell us a little bit about your company?* We are a financial advisory company for expatriates, providing medical insurance from a range of international and local providers, life insurance, general insurance, international investment and pension scheme.

*Which insurance companies do you represent?*

William Russell, Global Health, IMG, Bupa, IHI Bupa, Expacare, DKV, Nordic, IPH, and others.

*How should people decide which company to use?*

They inform us what they need and we advise them of their options, that meet their requirements

*What advice can you give to people looking to retire in Bali in deciding what kind of insurance cover they should use?*

They should have proper medical insurance (not simply travel insurance) at least for coverage of in-patient benefit and medical evacuation

*Is it possible for people just to use travel insurance and what are the potential problems of doing this?*

It is possible, however it will not be comprehensive enough to cover for medical treatment as it is designed for short term travel.

*Should people organize their health insurance before or after they arrive in Bali?*

They should have medical insurance when they arrive.

## *What if a person has pre-existing medical conditions?*

They should be upfront about their pre-existing conditions when they are applying for medical insurance by completing the medical questionnaire; pre-existing conditions is a question usually asked on the application form. The underwriter will then underwrite the information and will then revert back to applicant for the acceptance. The acceptance either offers to include the pre-existing condition and to offer cover or to exclude the pre-existing condition and not offer coverage or to offer it at a premium.

## *How does a person's age affect getting health insurance in Bali?*

Older people will be charged higher premiums compared to applicants below their age. In addition, there is a maximum limit for new applicants. For some providers, the maximum age limit is up to 74, and for others, the age is 64.

## *How can people make sure they are covered for motorbike or traffic accidents?*

Medical insurance covers accident treatment which occurs from a client's daily life and activity. However, for professional activity or work that involves risk it must be confirmed at the first inception to the insurance company, to ensure they are covered in those activities.

### How important is it to get emergency medical evacuation?

It is important as we never know when the required treatment will need to stabilize client's life or to get advance hospital treatment that is not available in Bali.

### Can you offer any other tips or advice for people thinking of retiring in Bali?

They should have proper medical treatment and organize a pension scheme fund.

Telephone: +62 21 769 2595
Email: bhfs@cbn.net.id
Web: www.bhfinancialservices.com

# Cost of living

One of reasons for deciding to live overseas for many westerners is the lower cost of living, particularly in developing regions like South East Asia and South America. While it is possible to live cheaper in Bali than many western countries, this is not always the case.

Bali is starting become more expensive. Real estate prices are going out of control, particularly in the south of Bali. Fortunately, it's still possible to find housing close to what locals might pay, but if you are looking for a beautiful villa with a swimming pool overlooking the beach, be prepared to pay for it. In areas popular with expats, there are plenty of homes in the million dollar plus range— yes dollars not rupiah!

Some people see the low salaries that people are paid in Bali and think that they might be able to live on a similarly low amount. The reality is that very few westerners could even dream of living on the same amount of money as a local person. You can of course live quite frugally by shopping at markets and cooking your own meals. Some people are happier living this way and some will be miserable. Shopping at local markets is a good way to experience the local way of life. You will need to bargain a bit, but it is also good for language practice. You also need to get up at the crack of dawn as there little or no refrigeration at traditional markets and they usually open and close early in the morning.

Tourism has also had a great affect on prices, as holidaying tourists generally have more money to spend and they are happy to splash it around freely. Restaurants and shops that are marketed towards tourists are generally more expensive. Many restaurants that cater to tourists also seem to add separate charges to the bill for service and tax. The concentration of these places in the south of Bali, means that the cost of living is more expensive than places with less tourists, like the north of Bali.

## Housing

As Bali becomes more popular with people wanting to have extended holidays, it is getting more difficult to find cheap deals. At the minimum, a simple two-bedroom house in the south of Bali will cost around US$500 a month. If you want your own pool or anything with the word 'villa' in it, you will expect to pay at least double this amount. In other parts of Bali, where there is less tourism, you can find much cheaper options. See the separate housing and accommodation section for more details.

## Food and drink

Most people reading this however, will probably spend most of their time shopping in supermarkets like Carrefour, Hardys and Lotte Mart, purely for the convenience and familiarity. All of these stores are reasonably well priced. The exception is imported food and ingredients. Indonesia puts high import taxes on imported food items. Usually, you can find a local equivalent but things like cheese, there aren't really any local products, so it's expensive to buy.

If you are not used to checking prices at supermarkets, it is a good time to start. I remember once picking up an imported brand of ground pepper one time and it was over 40,000 rupiah; I then found a local equivalent which cost around 5,000 rupiah. I am not really a penny pincher, but a couple of times when my grocery bill was higher than usual, I started looking more carefully at what things cost.

One of the biggest concerns some foreigners have about living in Bali is the high cost of imported alcohol. Indonesia has the largest Muslim population in the world, so it's fairly obvious that the situation is not going to change soon. You can expect to pay around double what you are used to for imported wine and spirits.

Bali produces some wine and it doesn't carry the import tax so it is cheaper. The wine is probably not going to win any international awards, but it is reasonable enough. Hatten Wines is the most well known brand. A locally produced wine "Two Islands" uses grapes imported from Australia, but is made in Bali, which makes it possible to get around the import tax.

It is hard to put an exact figure on grocery spending, but overall I would say that if you stick to fresh produce and locally made items, your food bill will probably be less than what you are likely to pay in Australia or Europe.

In Bali the water is not suitable for drinking, so another expense that you might not be used to paying for, is bottled water. A 19 liter drum of mineral water or *Aqua* costs around 10,000 rupiah. With the humidity, you will need to drink a lot more water than you are used to, so you tend to go through quite a bit.

## *Internet and communications*

Internet in Bali is quite expensive and the internet bill in the first house I rented, was more expensive than my rent! Telekom Speedy, which requires a telephone line, is the way many people use to access the internet in Bali. There are other ISPs available depending on where you are living.

Other ISPs that you might want to consider include:

Max3 – Offers fast internet, but their coverage is limited - http://www.max3.co.id/en/default.asp

Global Extreme – Has a wide area of coverage in southern Bali and you don't even need a phone line - www.globalxtreme.net

Blue Line – Offers high speed internet, mostly in the south of Bali, but also Ubud, Candidasa and even on Lembongan Island - www.blueline.co.id

### 3G Internet

Bali has a fairly good 3G network and is a great choice if are traveling or waiting to get internet installed at your house. You need to purchase a modem for about 400,000 rupiah and then you need to buy credit, like you do with a mobile phone. Find a modem that supports HSDPA, which is marketed as "3.5G".

It is a good idea not to buy a modem that is tied to a particular network, then you can chose a provider based on the price and coverage in your area.. The main providers include: Telekomsel Flash, "3," Simpati, XL, Axis, and Smart. Some networks work better than others in certain areas, so you can't really say which one is going to work best. If you are having problems with one network, you can easily buy a new SIM card for another network and try that.

## *Utilities*

It is difficult to say exactly how much you will spend on electricity. When I rented a small two-bedroom house, my electric bill was about 350,000 rupiah per month. That is for a small house with one AC running most of the time and with other typical appliances, like computers, refrigerator and television. The house had low wattage, so if you used appliances with high wattage, it inevitably cut the power. So every time I cooked a bit of toast, I would need to turn of the AC first. Foreigners building large villas with air-conditioning units in every room and other electric appliances, like a microwave and water heaters, will require higher wattage, which then also means a much higher electricity bill.

My water bill is about 50,000 rupiah a month. Gas is used for cooking and sometimes for hot water heaters. Most houses I have lived in have 15 kilo gas bottles that cost around 75,000 rupiah to fill. I cook most meals at home and you probably need to refill it once every two months.

## Transport

One important consideration you must have if you are thinking of living in Bali is transport. Any form of public transport is fairly limited in Bali. If you are in the south of Bali, you can usually find taxis everywhere. If you have been to Bali before, you will probably know that you should always try to take a BlueBird taxi. BlueBird taxis are generally very reliable. They will always turn on the meter and offer a professional service.

If you are traveling to other parts of the island the tour company Perama Tours (www.peramatour.com) offer a shuttle bus service between the main tourist centers across Bali and a ferry service to the Gili Islands.

If you want to experience how local people get around, you can take local buses almost anywhere around the island and further afield to Java. The buses cram people and luggage on and two people often occupy the space of a single seat. Buses also generally don't leave until they are full, so sometimes you need to be prepared for a long wait.

Motorbikes and scooters are popular with locals and expats alike. You can buy a second hand automatic Honda Vario for around 10 million rupiah. You can rent a similar bike for around 500,000 rupiah a month. A decent second hand car will cost around 100 million rupiah. Cars hold their values well in Bali, so provided you keep the car in good condition, you should be able to sell it for almost the same price as to what you bought it for after using it for a few years. Gasoline is subsidized by the government and is fixed at just 4,500 rupiah a liter!

## Staff costs

The minimum wage for a worker in Bali is around 1 million rupiah per month. The minimum is not enforced and many workers will earn much less than this. If you provide accommodation and meals for your staff, they may expect less. Paying a higher rate than the minimum wage can motivate your staff, but not always.

# Driver's license

If you plan on driving in Bali, whether it's a car or motorbike, you will need a valid driver's license. If you have a license in your own country, you should be able to get an International Driving Permit (IDP). It's proof that you have a driver's license in your own country and you need to carry it along with your original license. The permit is usually valid for one year in most countries. Some issuing authorities can create a new one for you and send it to you in Indonesia, or to a friends or family's address in your home country, who can then send it to you in Bali.

The other alternative is to get a local license or SIM (Surat Izin Mengemudi). If you've seen some of the way the locals drive in Bali, you probably wondered if anyone actually had a license! Many don't bother getting one, and sometimes you can see long lines of drivers before a police checkpoint waiting for the police to move on. Getting a license is more about filling in some forms and paying the fee than actually testing people's ability to drive.

Like with many bureaucratic processes in Indonesia, there's a fast way of doing things that's a little more expensive and the slow and tedious way, but cheaper. Getting a license is no exception, and if you know who to go to, the process will be a lot easier. Either way, you will need a valid KITAS, passport, driver's license from your home country and your Certificate of Police Registration (STM or Surat Tanda Melapor). For the south of Bali the testing center can be found at: Poltabes Denpasar on Jl. Gunung Sanghyang.

# Buying a car

If you hold a valid KITAS you can purchase a car in your own name. If you're staying in Bali long enough, say for a year or more, buying a car is a good option. Cars hold their value well, so if you buy a new car, you should be able to sell it for a good price several years later.

When buying a new car, the important documents you'll receive include:

- STNK (Surat Tanda Nomor Kendaraan). This is your car registration notice. You need to carry this document at all times while driving and is the document police will ask to see if they ever stop you.

- BPKB (Buku Pemilik Kendaraan Bermotor). This is the proof of ownership book and should be kept in a safe place and never in your car. If your car is stolen, and the thief has this book, they could potentially resell your car.

- Original invoice (Faktor)

- Receipt for the transaction (Kwitansi Pembayaran)

See here for more information on buying new and secondhand cars in Indonesia:

http://www.expat.or.id/info/buyingacar.html

A good place to find second hand cars for sale is the classified section of this website:

http://mobil.kapanlagi.com/

# Housing and finding accommodation

Finding suitable accommodation will be one of the biggest tasks you'll face when you first move to Bali. Some people may even prefer to find a house before they begin to move all of their personal belongings. Finding a place to live can be stressful in any country but if it's the first time you have lived overseas, it could be even more so.

If possible, try to give yourself as much time as possible to find a place. If you know the area you want to live in, find a comfortable hotel to stay in and book the room for 2-3 weeks. This will help you get to know the area better where you want to live and make some initial contacts. Most people's first choices for a location to live will be near where they have may have stayed on holidays. While the area might be convenient to spend your holidays, it could be a completely different feeling after you have decided to live there. Especially since the popular tourist areas are very busy and sometimes noisy.

Renting a house is going to be one of the first major financial decisions you make in Bali so it's important to try and remain calm and use the same sense of judgment when evaluating properties as you would in your home country. Sometimes people get all excited about the first property they see and find out later it has some problems or they over paid for it.

In general in Indonesia, you rent a house for at least one year and you need to pay the full year's rent in advance. If you find out later that there's a problem with the property and you decide to live elsewhere, it will be next to impossible to get your money back.

It's a good idea to also check out the area your house is in at night, before you sign any contracts or pay a deposit. Some houses are quiet during the day, but at night are very noisy because they are close to a karaoke bar, or some other kind of late night entertainment venue. Karaoke bars in Bali are typically fronts for prostitution, and usually the owners will have contacts with the police so there's no way to complain about the noise.

If you are from the United States, you will be disappointed to know that Bali does not have a MLS (Multiple Listing Service). For non-Americans the MLS is a centralized database of properties which enables prospective renters or buyers to get a full list of properties that match their requirements. Most real estate agents in Bali guard their listings from other agents and it is fairly rare for agents to cooperate and share information. This means you will need to visit as many agents as possible.

You may even find the same property listed with multiple agents, all at different prices. Sometimes agents in Bali work out a price with the seller and then they make the price higher and the agent then pockets the difference, on top of the agreed commission. This makes it important to visit as many agents as possible, as you could be able to get the same property for a cheaper price.

There are few different ways you can go about finding a house to rent.

- Using the internet
- Property listings in the Bali Advertiser (www.baliadvertiser.biz)
- Using an agent
- Finding a place directly from the owner
- Asking expat friends and locals for help

I would suggest not limiting yourself to one method. All of the methods have their advantages and disadvantages. Using the internet is a good way to get started, especially if you are still in your home country and want to start getting an idea of property prices. Not all agents and property owners, however, are computer or internet savvy. The ones that are, tend to over price their properties. Rumah123 (www.rumah123.com) is a website aimed at Indonesians so prices seem more reasonable.

Indonesia doesn't have any special education or licensing requirements for real estate agents so basically anyone can call themselves an agent. Some of the more established agents will have an office and staff. There are some foreign real estate franchises in Bali, such as Ray White (www.raywhite.co.id). Some other places you can find property include Olx Classifieds website (denpasar.olx.co.id/en/houses-apartments-for-rent-cat-363), which has listings for Denpasar, Kuta, Ubud and Singaraja.

The owner generally pays the fees to the real estate agent. So if you are asked by the agent for any money at any time, it's probably better to find someone else. There are some reliable and trustworthy agents—the problem is finding them! If you ask for recommendations from people they will generally just tell you about properties they know of themselves. Everyone likes playing agent in Bali, both locals and expats, so be aware that your well meaning friend who shows you some properties, they could be getting a commission themselves! While this is not necessarily a problem in itself, it is something to keep in mind.

In Australia and in most western countries it's typical for most people to use agents whether they are buying or renting a house. In Bali, however, using an agent is more of an exception than the rule. I don't know the exact reason for it, maybe owners don't like having to pay fees to the agents and they think they can manage everything by themselves.

So what you often find in Bali, is owners simply putting up a sign at the front of their house with a mobile number to call. If it is in Indonesian, Di Jual is 'for sale' and Di Sewakan is 'for rent'. The owner may put up the price if a foreigner calls, so it might be an idea to get a local friend to make the initial contact.

There is some perception that finding property this way you can get something cheaper because you are cutting out the 'middle man', in this case, an agent. This can happen, but not always. I do know of a property for example where someone paid more for a house when they went to the owner directly than what it was being listed for with an agent. By dealing directly with the owner you can sometimes get a bargain, but at the same time, you might also end up overpaying.

## *Checking out the property*

Generally speaking, the tenants pay for any ongoing maintenance in Bali so it is very important to check everything with the house before you pay any money or sign any contracts. If the owner advertises that the house has hot water and air conditioning you should turn them on and check that they are working satisfactorily.

Turn on the taps and check that there is good pressure in the water. Smell the water, without drinking it. If your house gets its water from a bore or well, the water can sometimes have a problem, like being too close to a septic tank. Check the wattage of the house also, especially if you want to run several high wattage appliances at the same time. One house we rented didn't have much power, and you couldn't have two high wattage appliances on at the same time. So if you wanted to cook some toast, first you had to switch off the air-conditioner!

Another thing to watch out for are pre-paid meters. These are meters where you need to purchase credit in advance for your electricity. I have never had one in Bali, but I did have a pre-paid meter when I was living in China and it was a right old pain in the neck having to buy credit all of the time. If you run out of credit during a weekend, you could be sitting in the dark until Monday morning to buy more credit.

If the house has a pool, be sure to check the filter and that all of the equipment is working fine. Pools are great to have in Bali, but you do need to be aware of the ongoing maintance costs and the cost for chemicals.

If there are any problems, you could ask the owner to fix them before you begin the contract. Many houses for example have leaky roofs, which will be a big problem in the rainy season. Check for water patches in the ceiling; this is a good sign the house has a leaky roof.

Termites are a big problem in Bali. Check the windows and door frames for termites by tapping it with a screwdriver or something similar. Termites build pencil sized tubes of dirt which they use to travel. If you see any such tubes around the wood work, your house could have a problem with termites. It is probably a bigger issue if you are buying the house, but if you are entering into a long term contract, it is still worth checking out. On the surface the wood might look fine, but the inside could all be eaten away.

## *Bargaining on the price*

Like most things in Indonesia, property prices are open for negotiation. From my own experience with property in Australia, the market price of one property generally depends on similar sales or rentals of another property and owners generally follow the guidance of an agent in setting the price. Unfortunately property doesn't seem to operate this way in Bali. You could have one house for rent for 15 million per year and the neighboring house is on the market for 27 million per year, even though the two houses are basically identical!

The other anomaly I have found when renting property in Bali is that owners have a price in their mind that they will not even consider going below. They would prefer to let the property sit vacant until they find a tenant willing to pay the price they want. It can sometimes be a frustrating experience.

## Things to check before signing lease

The first thing you need to check is who actually owns the property. Sometimes people trying to rent a house don't actually own it and are looking to sublet it. If this is the case, you may need to get permission from the owner. Try to view a copy of the original land certificate and check the name on it. Compare it to the owner's ID card (KTP).

If the person is married, make sure their partner also agrees to you renting their house, to avoid problems later. I know of a case where the husband was willing to rent their house, but his wife wasn't in agreement and wanted a lot more money for the house.

It's a good idea to use the services of a notary to create a proper rental agreement and to get it signed by all parties, especially if you are dealing directly with the owner. The fee is a small amount for the extra protection it provides. If the owner is not willing to make an agreement with a notary, even if you agree to pay all of the fees, there could be a problem with the property.

Most of the time, you will need to pay the electric and water bills yourself. However, if you rent a higher end property, the utility bills could be included. Ask the owner for the latest receipts for electricity and water payments. Sometimes owners neglect paying the bill and then when pay your first bill, you may also get lugged in with paying the previous month's bill, and good luck trying to get the money back from the landlord.

## Paying Utilities

For electricity, readings are taken of your meter every month and posted to your account on the 6th and then you have until the 24th of each month to pay your bill. You don't receive a bill in the mail like in most countries, but you need to find out how much you need to pay yourself and then pay the required amount.

Fortunately, now you can check out how much you need to pay by checking the PLN (electricity provider) website: www.pln.co.id by entering your 12 digit account number.

Bills can be paid at the PLN office, but there are also many shops around Bali that also accept payments. Look for the sign "Bayar Listrik Di Sini". You can also pay through ATMs and online banking through most Indonesian banks, such as BCA.

If you have town water you can pay your water bill at the local PDAM office.

# Buying property in Bali

To buy or to rent?  Even if you have made up your mind to buy property in Bali, I would strongly suggest renting for at least 6 months to a year.  This will give you time to get to know the area well, make contacts with contractors and get a good feeling for the prices.

Renting has its advantages—you don't have to deal with foreign ownership issues, no large capital outlay, and it is easy to move to another place.  The downside is that it's not going to feel like it's your own home, so you are less likely to want to make any improvements to it.  The owner of the house could sell it, so you might be forced to move at some stage.

Foreigners cannot own property in their own name in Indonesia and this is unlikely to change in the near future.  If you weren't already aware of this law, you would probably be surprised if you came to Bali, because of all of the property advertisements and real estate agent offices that only seem to be marketing their properties for sale to tourists and expats visiting Bali.

So if foreigners cannot legally own property in Indonesia, how do these real estate agents operate?  Foreign ownership of property in Indonesia is a complicated and very contentious issue.  It is extremely important to get independent and professional advice if you are looking to buy property in Bali.  The following is a basic introduction to some of the issues surrounding foreign property ownership in Indonesia.

In no way is this meant to be taken as legal advice and it should only enforce my point even further about getting professional legal advice.

## Using a nominee

Since you cannot have the property in your own name, some foreigners opt for putting the property in an Indonesian person's name. There are obvious pitfalls in doing this and stories abound of foreigners who have had problems using this method.

Even with the risks involved, it is still a common way for foreigners to buy property in Indonesia. Without a doubt you need to have someone you can trust. Your notary will make agreements between yourself and the nominee making it very difficult or next to impossible for your nominee to sell the property without your knowledge. If the relationship with the nominee ever turns sour while the nominee may not be able to sell the property, they can make life difficult for you. The difficulty then is if you ever need to take the case to court. What chance do you have of winning your case since the law does not allow foreign ownership of freehold property in the first place?

## Buying property with an Indonesian spouse

A big shock to me when I started researching living in Indonesia, was when I found out that if an Indonesian citizen marries a foreigner, they actually lose the right to own property in Indonesia. The problem I believe is that because of joint ownership laws in marriages in Indonesia, when a foreigner marries an Indonesian person, the foreigner in effect will jointly own any currently owned property or property bought in the future by the Indonesian partner.

Admittedly, the whole issue is a grey area, and many Indonesian-foreign couples own property in Indonesia. One of the most common "solutions" to get around this is for a couple to create a pre-nuptial agreement before they are married, stating that the foreigner will not have any rights to the property bought by the Indonesian spouse.

## Long term lease

The long term lease is a good option for foreigners, as they can have the lease written up using their own name. The standard term is 25 years, but you can have extensions to this included in your agreements. Again, it is important to have a good notary to create the lease and of course you need to do just as much due diligence on the property as if you were buying it. You need to also consider what happens to the lease in the event you die.

## Access to your property

Whether you are using a nominee or a long term lease, it is important to know what access you have to your property. You need to make sure that the gang or lane to your property is a public road. So many foreigners have been caught without public access to their land, and if you wait until it's too late the owner of the land the road runs through can basically charge you whatever they want to cross their land.

## Building a house

Buying an existing house is a good idea. Even if might require some renovation, it is going to be  much less stressful than building a brand new home. Horror stories abound about how people lost  large amounts of money building their dream house in Bali.  The stories are not limited to problems with local builders either, but foreign builders as well.

If you still want to build your own house, I strongly recommend that you stay in Bali during the construction and you visit the project on a daily basis. Do not even attempt to try and manage the build remotely, even if you have a trusted "friend" who is willing to offer to help you. Spend as much time as you can choosing a builder, ask for references and make sure you check other projects they have completed.

Some people prefer to manage the build themselves. Buying the materials and hiring the workers. Again this has its advantages and disadvantages. I wouldn't recommend this option unless you have building experience. The way Balinese build their houses is more than likely completely different from what you are probably used to. Trying to explain how you want your house built to a builder who only knows one way to build is not going to be easy, even if you can speak fluent Indonesian. Be prepared to lose some hair if decide to go down this path!

Balinese workers are usually very diligent and highly skilled in their own way. There is no apprenticeship system in Indonesia so workers only learn by doing and from other workers or their family. You do, however, need to spend as much time as possible watching their work.

Get a building permit (IMB) before you start doing any building and get proper design drawings made up. The permit should specify exactly what materials and fittings will be included in the price. The quality of fixtures can also vary a great deal so it is important to also specify exactly what brands of fittings you will be using.

Create a payment schedule which relates directly to the percentage of completion of the build. You don't want to get in a situation where 80 percent of the money has been paid, while only 40 percent of the project is complete. Insist on your builder providing a written guarantee.

There is a regular building column in the Bali Advertiser called "Fixed Abode", written by an expat builder. It is a great source of information for anyone building, renovating or even just maintaining a house in Bali. If you are doing any kind of construction in Bali, I would strongly suggest going back and reading all of the articles, which you can find on their website: http://www.baliadvertiser.biz. There are many things that you have to deal with in Bali that you might never have considered in your home country, such as water tanks and termites.

## *Ten tips for building or renovating a house in Bali*

1.  Create a budget for your project and project schedule. Factor in any major ceremonies that may take place during the schedule, where work will likely stop, such as a Galungan.

2.  Be prepared for possible increases in the budget and factor in price increases of materials.

3.  If you are building a house, or won't be living in the house while you are renovating, employ a security guard to watch your materials and house at night.

4.  Get references from your builder or contractor. Get a detailed quote and question all costs and calculations. Many builders will under price their quote, just to get the job.

5.  Make sure you can communicate well with your builder or project manager, or hire someone who can translate for you.

6.  Be on site and supervise your workers as much as possible. Even if you are employing a project manager or experienced builder, you don't need to be an expert to see where there might be problems.

7.  Monitor your workers and laborers and make sure they are actually on site and you are not paying wages for people who never even show up. Salaries are paid on a weekly basis in cash. Make sure your workers sign a confirmation that they received their salary.

8.  Get all the receipts for material purchases and make sure the amounts are correct when they are delivered. It is easy for builders to divert some of materials you paid for to another job that they might be working on.

9. Monitor the quality of the materials you are buying. It is common for people to pay for higher quality materials only to have inferior materials delivered to your project.

10. Try to use local workers as much as possible and buy your materials locally. This is especially the case outside of the main tourist areas where employment prospects are more limited. It is a great way to show support to the local community which you will be moving into.

# Employing Staff

Along with visas, the topic of employing household staff would have to be the most common conversation topic amongst expats in Bali. Many of the stories are usually about the maid who went on holiday and never came back and maids who broke electrical appliances because they didn't know how to use them.

Even for middle class families in Indonesia it is fairly common for people to employ maids or a *pembantu*. One of the requirements for the retirement visa is that you agree to employ at least one person to help you in your home. Some people also employ a driver, security and a cook.

It can sometimes take a while to find someone who is suitable for your needs. For many people the maids also become part of the family. A maid can live in your house or in their own place and then commute every day.

For people from some countries where it is not common to employ household staff, it can take some time to get used to having another person living in their house. Some people prefer their maid to start work in the morning and continue on until the afternoon or early evening.

It is important to try and set some guidelines from the beginning, including the working hours and the tasks your staff are expected to perform. Initially it might be a good idea to find someone through an agency in Bali, so if there is a problem, it will be easier to deal with.

Here are some agencies that advertise in the Bali Advertiser, that you might want to consider using.

Bali Krisna Service - www.balikrisnaservice.com

Queen Agency – 081 337 328 401

Bali Employment Agency – 0361 8839741
baliemploymentagency@hotmail.com

Finding someone through friends and colleagues is another common way
of finding staff and is  common in Indonesia.  Try to find out as much as
possible about the person, their background, experience and family.  You
might need to teach your staff how to operate the electrical appliances in
your home.

If you have a dog or other pet, you need to know if your staff will be
comfortable with them.  Muslims may not want to live or work in a house
with a dog.  Even many Balinese are afraid of dogs.

It is important to agree to a salary and when payments will be made.
Record everything in a book and ask your staff to sign it each time they are
paid.  Many employers also pay for health insurance for their staff.

# Moving your household goods

From reading various expat forums, there seems to be a strong tendency for many people once they have decided to retire in Bali, to pack up everything and ship it. While on one hand this is understandable as many people have sentimental items that they couldn't bear living without. On the other hand, with the high cost of shipping all of your personal possessions and the possibility of having to pay custom fees, it can sometimes make sense to sell or give away almost everything you own, or put it all into storage and start a fresh when you move to Bali.

White goods and electrical items are reasonably priced in Bali and most major brands can be found. Indonesia uses 220 volts 50 Hz, so any electrical items you bring need to run on that. You can also get beautiful custom made furniture made in Bali rather inexpensively, so it seems rather pointless trying to ship bulky furniture over. Bed sizes are more than likely different to your home country, so it's best to buy sheets in Bali, or even better, get them custom made.

For many people their most sentimental items are photos and home videos. They can be bulky and not easy to transport, not to mention what would happen if they got lost or damaged in the move. One idea is to get all of your old, videos and music collections and save them all to a computer hard disk or external drive and keep the originals with family or put them in storage.

Sea freight is cheaper than air freight, but your goods may arrive in Jakarta or Surabaya in Java and then you will then need to get them transported to Bali. With air freight you are going to pay a little more, but at least they will arrive quicker and you can easily go and pick them up yourself at the airport.

Here is a list of some possible cargo companies to contact:

Jetta (www.jetta.com.au) – Australian based company that provides an excess baggage service.

Santa Fe (www.santaferelo.com) – Relocation service company.

# Where to live in Bali

Once you have decided that you will live in Bali, the next big decision you will have to make is where exactly you want to live in Bali. Where you want to live will be based on what kinds of things you enjoy doing and what kind of lifestyle you want. If you like bars and nightclubs for example, you will want to be close to the action in Kuta or Seminyak.

If you have been to Bali before, you probably have some idea of which part you would like to live in. If you are thinking of living in the south of Bali, I would suggest that you at least give some consideration to living somewhere other than the south. At least in my opinion, there are so many more nicer places in Bali and you are still a short drive away from everything the south has to offer.

Here are some questions you might want to ask yourself to help narrow down the decision.

- Do you want to live by the sea or in the mountains?
- Do you want a quiet lifestyle in a village or do you want to be in an urban area?
- Do you want to live in areas with lots of other expats?
- What kinds of activities or sports do you like?
- Do you need to be close to a hospital that can provide care for westerners?
- Are you comfortable living in an area where English might not be understood?
- Do you want to live in an area with a large variety of western restaurants or bars?

## *The south*

The south of Bali is where most of the action takes place. It's close to the international airport, and the administrative capital of Bali, Denpasar. It is a busy place and there's always something happening. It is often the first choice for people to visit or even live in Bali. It has the worst traffic in Bali and suffers from the same problems of many popular tourist destinations where the infrastructure has not kept up with the growth.

The south of Bali has the best choice of restaurants and places to go out. It's popular with surfers and partygoers. It also has the best shopping and medical facilities on the island. The popularity also makes it generally more expensive than other parts of Bali.

## Seminyak

Seminyak is a popular place with tourists and expats. It is the 'cool' place to be seen in Bali. It is the home of many high end boutiques, villas and nightclubs and even has its own magazine, *The Yak*. Prices for housing and living costs in general are the highest in Bali, especially if you want to be close to the beach.

## Kerobokan

Kerobokan is most famous for its jail, where many westerners are doing time for drug smuggling. While you don't want to end up in the jail, Kerobokan has slightly more affordable housing options than neighboring Seminyak and is still just a short drive to the beach.

# Canggu

Just as Seminyak sprung up as Kuta and Legian became more crowded, villas and hotels are moving further northwest into Canggu. Canngu is located north of Seminyak along the way to Tanah Lot. It includes the villages of Berawa and Cemagi and is popular with surfers. It is also home to the exclusive 'Canggu Club' (http://www.cangguclub.com).

# Sanur

Sanur is becoming a popular place for families and retirees. It has a more laid back feel to it compared to Kuta and Seminyak. It also has a very wide selection of eating options and places to stay. One of the things I love is the beachside walking/jogging/cycling track, which runs for about 5km. Property located between the bypass highway and the beach are the most popular, and prices have really started to skyrocket. If you don't mind living on the "other side" of the bypass, you can find some good deals. Sanur also has many "cafes" which are basically brothels and feature loud karaoke music at night. Be sure any house you buy or rent is not near these "entertainment" areas.

# Bukit

The Bukit is the southern most point of Bali and is a limestone peninsula with most of the coastline featuring dramatic cliff drops to the ocean. The views are spectacular, but it is a very dry area to live. The Nusa Dua area is well known for its many five star hotels and resorts, but there also housing areas for locals and expats.

# Jimbaran

Jimbaran is famous for its seafood restaurants catering to tourists located right on the beach. It is a popular area for expats and still only a short drive to the airport. It is possible to find some reasonably priced rentals in Jimbaran.

## *Central Bali*

# Ubud

Ubud has quite a large expat population and it is regarded as the cultural heart of Bali. Painters, musicians, and yoga practitioners all flock to Ubud. While the main center of Ubud has become busy with large buses, it is still possible to stay in quiet villages far removed from the tourist hoards. Ubud has become even more popular after the *Eat, Pray, Love* book and movie was released. This has pushed up the prices for rentals and property in general. Ubud is a little cooler than the coastal regions of Bali and gets a lot of rain, keeping it lush and green. With the large number of expats and tourists visiting Ubud, there is an excellent range of local and international restaurants.

## *East Coast*

The east coast of Bali is much quieter than the south and there are many great places to live along the coast. Candidasa and its surrounding areas are becoming popular places to live. The roads to the south are also improving, making it quicker to reach the airport and shopping centers in the south.

## North Coast

The north coast includes Bali's second largest city and former capital, Singaraja. Lovina is gaining popularity, particularly with European expats. Property and housing prices are a fraction of what you pay in the south - at least for now. Beach front property prices are becoming very expensive, but you can also get reasonably priced land in the hills behind Lovina with beautiful sea views.

# Visas

One of the most common discussions amongst expats are visa issues. This section discusses the various visa options you have for staying in Bali. Of course this guide is for people retiring in Bali, so the retirement visa is the obvious choice for most people, but I also wanted to mention some of the other visas that are available, that you might find more suitable depending on your circumstances.

## *Should I even bother getting a retirement visa?*

There are some real costs involved in getting a retirement visa, and some people might be wondering if there other options for staying in Bali without getting the retirement visa. In the end it depends on how much time you want to spend dealing with immigration and the number of times you want to be doing 'visa runs' ie, leaving and entering the country just to get a new visa and also how long you plan on staying in Bali.

The advantage of going to the trouble of getting a retirement visa is that you have better legal status for staying in the country. The main advantages are being able to open a bank account, buy a car or motorbike in your own name and get a local driver's license. You can renew the visa every year and you don't have to bother with having to leave the country just to get a new visa.

If you are on a visa that only allows you to stay a few months at a time, it might be cheaper than the retirement visa, just in visa costs, but if you factor in the cost of flights and accommodation to leave the country and get a new visa, the retirement visa will probably save you money in the long run in terms of both time and hassle. Also, with a social visa you need to renew it every month and it will always be on your mind, when you have to renew.

## Tourist visas

If you are planning on staying for just a month or two at a time, you might want to consider just staying on a tourist visa. A visa on arrival (VOA) is valid for one month and can be extended for another 30 days, for a maximum stay of 60 days.

## Social visa

The social visa is intended for people wanting to visit Indonesia to visit family or friends. The reality is that it's often used by people who might have the means to retire in Bali but have not reached the required age for the retirement visa.

You need to apply for the visa outside of Indonesia and you need an Indonesian friend to be your sponsor. You need a copy of their identity card (KTP) and a sponsor letter. There is a sample sponsor letter provided in Appendix A. Your sponsor should have an address in Bali, if you plan on living in Bali, otherwise you could have trouble when you do the renewals.

The visa is initially valid for 2 months and can then be renewed each month, four times, for a maximum stay of 6 months. If you have all of the documentation, you can easily get the visa through an agent in Singapore. The renewal cost is around IDR 250,000 if you do it yourself. If you do it through an agent, it will cost around IDR 600,000 - 700,000 for each renewal. Doing the extension yourself requires several trips to the immigration office, so while it can save you money, it can be time consuming.

Here are the contact details of a couple of visa agents in Singapore:

**Ismail Visa Service**

190 Clemenceau Avenue #02-16
Singapore Shopping Centre
Singapore 239924
Office telephone: (65) 6334 5520
Mobile: 9636 4854
Fax No: (65) 6334 5518

**Malik Yusof**
Mobile: 96753307
Email: malksav@hotmail.com
Fax: 64549984

## *Retirement Visa requirements*

If you are serious about retiring in Bali, like renting or leasing a house for an extended period and want to be able to be able to open a bank account in your own name, getting the retirement visa is highly recommended.

The retirement visa is valid for 5 years and the KITAS is valid for 1 year, but can be extended five times. The code for the visa which you might see it written in places is 'Index 319'. After five years, the process just starts again.

The requirements for the visa include:

- Aged 55 years or over
- Copy of passport with at least 18 months of validity

- Copy of marriage certificate (if married)
- Proof of funds showing income from a pension or similar income of at least US$1,500 per month or US$18,000 a year.
- Copy of health insurance
- Four passport photos 4 x 6 cm
- Statement declaring the employment of an Indonesian maid/servant

A visa company needs to sponsor you for the visa, so you need to employ an agency to sponsor you and they will do all of the leg work for you to get the visa.

After five years, you can then apply for a permanent stay visa which is referred to as a KITAP.

It is difficult to recommend one agent over another. I have heard many good and bad stories about many of the different visa agents in Bali. I interviewed three of most popular agents which you can find in Appendix B.

## *Exit permit*

When you depart from Indonesia, and you are on a KITAS, you will be required to get an exit/re-entry permit. If you don't get an exit permit and leave the country, you will need to reapply for the retirement visa again. Exit permits are not required for tourist or social visas. Previously there were single entry and multiple entry exit permits, but now you can only get a multiple entry permit. The permit is stamped into your passport. I would suggest getting the permit as soon as you get your KITAS, in case you have to leave Bali in an emergency, such as for medical reasons or to visit family. It can sometimes take a few days to process the permit, so it is a good idea to be prepared to leave in an emergency situation.

# Interviews

## *Retirement blogging*

The following is an interview I did with Vyt Karazija. Vyt writes a weekly column for the Bali Times about his experiences living in Bali and is great for a dose of laughter. You can read an archive of his articles on his blog: http://borborigmus.wordpress.com

*Can you please start by telling me how you became interested in Bali?*

I started visiting Bali regularly about 12 years before deciding to live here. During that time, I became gradually more and more aware of Bali's possibilities as a place to live, rather than just visit.

*There are several different countries that offer retirement visa programs, can you tell me, what made you decide on Bali?*

I decided on Bali basically because of my familiarity with the place as a tourist. I also was attracted to the people, the culture, and the way that Bali embraces Pancasila as a genuine, heartfelt philosophy rather than the political football it seems to be some in other parts of Indonesia. Bottom line–I felt comfortable here.

*Did you spend much time looking at other possible retirement destinations?*

Thailand was one possibility, but I discounted it because for one thing, I have never been there, and for another, the unstable political situation worried me. Malaysia was another possibility, and its expat program seemed attractive at first. However, I felt that for me, the increasingly fundamentalist mindset there, plus my personal perception of government rigidity made it less desirable than Bali. I considered Singapore briefly, but felt that there was little point in moving from one highly-regulated environment to another. Vietnam was another option, but would need a lot more research before I would make that shift.

*Most people who live in Bali say that it is a very different experience than just coming for holiday. What has been your experience and what do you think are the main differences.*

I couldn't agree more. From my first day as an expat here, I felt different. For one thing, I wasn't just here to party and/or unwind–as a resident, there are heaps of things that must be done here–just as many as there would be living back 'home'. For example, I needed to arrange long-term accommodation, hire and manage staff (not an affectation, but a condition of one's residency permit), and source transport. Ongoing things include paying household bills, making an attempt to become proficient in the language, and beginning to understand the complex drivers of society here. Then of course there is the need to deal with the residency permit paperwork that must be renewed each year and can take months to process …

I also found a need to develop a new identity, one based on being a *guest* in this country instead of believing that I, as an expat, actually *belong* here. I don't believe any bule can 'belong' here; our presence is tolerated, perhaps even welcomed by some for our economic benefits, but we will never a part of the core culture of Bali. I am fortunate enough to feel like a welcome guest, but I would never succumb to the illusion that I am any more than a guest.

My experience has been positive, perhaps because I am happy (in the main) to go with the flow.

## VISAS

*Can you please explain how you went about applying for the retirement visa?*

After looking at doing the whole process myself and finding out just what a convoluted maze it is, I decided to use an immigration agent. It cost me about 6.8 million rupiah to set up the whole deal, which included processing of all the documentation and any necessary hand-holding when I first arrived.

I came to Bali on a 'final' visit a month or so before moving here permanently. It was easier to initiate the process here and to be walked through what needed to be done back in Australia during the final month. This visit was also necessary to locate accommodation and sign a lease (a signed lease document is part of the documentation you need to apply). A stack of other conditions needed to be met as well, and some of these were much easier to arrange in Bali.

Then, it was back to Australia, because the 1-year visa I needed (in my case known as a Retirement KITAS) can only be applied for while you are out of Indonesia. In the meantime, all documentation was sent to Jakarta for processing. This can take a month or more. Eventually, the Jakarta Immigration authorities send a letter of approval to the Indonesian Embassy in your closest capital city in Australia. Then you need to go there to *apply* for the actual visa (but only on certain days and times) and come back in a week (on a *different* day and time) to pick it up.

The stamp which they put into the passport was *not* a KITAS, it was a 'VITAS'. I then had to enter Indonesia within 30 days of its issue, or face starting from scratch. Once in Bali, I had to report to the immigration office within 5 days to have my VITAS converted to a KITAS. This took about 2 weeks, during which time Immigration retained my passport. Careful planning was essential, because there are lots of things which must be done on arrival that require a passport–and of course, the immigration authorities have that.

Oh, I also made sure I applied for and got the "Multiple Entry & Exit" endorsement. It allows you to come and go from Indonesia as you please. Without it, if you leave the country, even after a fortnight, your Retirement KITAS expires instantly and you have to start the KITAS application circus all over again ...

*There are many different agents offering visa services, how did you go about selecting your agent?*

I ignored all the ads for a start, and talked to expats here instead - people who had already been through the mill and could give me recommendations. After that, I spoke personally to a couple of agents and trusted my gut instincts, moderated by a healthy dose of skepticism. I chose the one who seemed most knowledgeable and was up-front about all the fees and charges involved. She turned out to be excellent and has provided consistently good service for 2 subsequent renewals.

**Knowing about the process now, would you do anything differently?**

Not a thing. There is very little that I can do differently anyway, as the process is tightly controlled by the Immigration authorities. There is the option of flying solo without an agent, which is considerably cheaper. However, I believe that the potential for problems - such as slow response times, so-called "irregularities" with documentation (which can usually solved by paying an exorbitant 'facilitation fee') and the fact that most official forms here are in formal Bahasa Indonesia - are just too great for me not to use an agent.

### *MAKING THE MOVE*

*Can you describe how you shipped your personal belongings to Bali? How was the experience?*

I didn't take all that much, cramming as much as I could into the allowable luggage limit on my flight. The rest I sent as "Unaccompanied Baggage", which arrived on a flight 5 days later. I went to collect it, had to show my passport, had the luggage minutely scrutinised by Customs, and was forced to pay nearly 1,000,000 rupiah for 'duty' on an old desktop computer worth maybe 30,000 rupiah.

I was lucky. Friends who arrived 12 months later to join me here sent their belongings via a cargo company. These were to arrive in Surabaya and were to be trucked to Bali. While in transit, Jakarta changed the rules. All expat personal belongings now required an 'Import Licence" and huge "Import Duties" to be paid. The friends tried to get the required import licence. "No, only companies can apply", was the response. When they said they had a company, they were then told that the company had to have 'warehousing space' of at least 25,000 square metres to be eligible to apply.

There followed a series of demands for constantly varying 'import duties', which they refused to pay on the basis that since the goods had not yet officially entered the country, these fees were therefore illegal. Then they were told that the goods are now attracting 'storage charges'. Eventually they were informed that the goods would be destroyed or sold. Eventually, the goods were shipped back to Australia after 6 months.

The whole episode considerably soured my friend's view of Indonesian officialdom. This was in 2010 - maybe things are better now.

*Do you remember before you moved to Bali that you had any big concerns or worries? And how did you resolve those concerns?*

Having been here frequently and done considerable research, I was not all that worried. However, what I hadn't anticipated was the level of passive aggression towards expats on the part of the central Government. Indonesia is not all that expat-friendly, but in my personal situation, most issues were dealt with a minimum of angst. I know that I may, or may not get my KITAS renewed each year - there is no real security here for expats - but that is the nature of the game here, and I will just accept changed circumstances as they arise.

However, if I had school-age children, I might regard some issues as more serious. The same friend who had the 'personal belongings' problem also fell foul of the central government's incomprehensible tendency to change the rules of the game without warning. Mid-way through a school year, the Jakarta administration decided arbitrarily to change 'Student KITAS' regulations, suddenly raising the minimum age to 17. My friend's son, who was 13, was refused a Student visa - because he was now 'too young'. As his International School required a Student KITAS as a condition of enrolment, he could not continue attending.

At the same time, the authorities refused visa extensions for a significant number of teachers at his school, ostensibly because there were too many foreign teachers employed, and that those jobs should go to locals. With the consequent uncertainty in educational options, my friend reluctantly left Bali and returned to Australia after only one year.

If I had a business here, I would be more worried - the level of corruption, the extortion attempts and other impediments to profitable business existence (not to mention the ever-present risk of your local 51% partner deciding to abscond with your wealth) would, for me, make it a dicey proposition. Luckily, my Retirement Visa does not allow me to work or run a business, so that question is moot.

Should I have entertained the idea of getting married to a local in Indonesia (which is as likely as getting kicked to death by a duck), I would have worried about another insane law passed last year. Foreign men who want to marry a Muslim woman must pay the Government a $50,000 USD "marriage bond". This law was passed, but no-one knows whether it was ever actually implemented. As far as I know, it's still on the books.

The short answer is that I have no significant concerns for myself as a retiree (except for the constant uncertainty of getting my KITAS extended), but I believe that expats with different circumstances should do some serious research before coming here.

### *CULTURE*

**Did you study much about Balinese culture before you came here?**

I read up a little, although I have found that some of the published information is somewhat out of date. Bali is a diverse, changing and vibrant culture, and there can be many regional differences in the way that things are done. Things that are sometimes regarded as traditional Balinese customs, for example, the Kecak dance, are actually recent innovations by foreigners.

**If so, do you have any advice for people to learn more about Balinese culture?**

My own view is to avoid self-professed 'experts', particularly if they are not Balinese. I have found that talking to ordinary Balinese locals seems to give me a more coherent overview of how things work here, and what the main drivers of society seem to be. But there are so many levels within levels here, that I will always remain an intrigued outsider, hopefully learning more each day.

## GOVERNMENT

*When I did a survey of people who were considering retiring in Bali, "government stability" or instability was a common concern for many people. What are your feelings and experience on this?*

Government stability in Bali itself is not really an issue. The place is chaos personified, so the actions of government leaders here seem to be ignored by practically everyone, being treated as background noise. Rarely do any local decisions here impact on expats.

The stability of the National government is more of a problem. Issues concerning visas, immigration, importation of goods and personal possessions, alcohol taxes, blasphemy laws, pornography laws and the like are all controlled by the Central Government. The ruling coalition is heavily in the thrall of Islamist interests and many laws and regulations are aimed at majority Muslim sensibilities, yet are still applied to Bali, which has only a 9% Muslim presence. This causes tensions. The National Government has also been known to have a strongly nationalistic streak, which means that the interests of expats are often well off its radar, except when expats can be gouged for even more money.

Government lawmakers also tend to pass laws with little regard, or even understanding, of their consequences for anyone, but especially Bali. The ramifications for expats are often unexpected and can be distressing. Laws are sometimes passed, then rescinded, or passed and never implemented. Religion dominates, and the fact the Indonesia is a secular democracy often seems to be forgotten. Corruption is endemic.

In my view, all this results in there being a deeply unstable government in Jakarta, which means a very fluid environment for expats living in Bali as a result.

*Another concern people had about moving to Bali is corruption in the government and police.*
*What has been your experience and do you think it is something for people who are thinking to retire in Bali, need to be concerned about?*

I think corruption is widespread throughout Indonesia, and Bali is no

109

exception. As anywhere, power and influence can let you by-pass most laws and regulations. If you are short on those two, the ubiquitous exchange of money for favours here comes a close second. There is major corruption here which sometimes borders on extortion, and that worries me, even though I have not yet been directly impacted.

However, I think the widespread *minor* corruption here should be taken in context. If I break a traffic law, I pay a fine both in Australia and in Bali. The difference is, in Australia, the fine goes to consolidated revenue for the government to waste as it sees fit. Here my 'fine' goes towards providing food for a cop who is paid $120 per month salary, and simply can't support a family on that wage. I don't have a problem with that.

Things are not quite as black and white in Bali as they might be elsewhere …

## COST OF LIVING

***How do you find the cost of living in Bali and how does it compare with your home country?***

It's substantially less, although Bali is not the super-cheap place it is reputed to be. Accommodation costs substantially less, which for me means a better quality place than I could afford in Australia. Very high-cost accommodation is also available, especially from non-local owners. Shopping around is always a good idea. Electricity costs are similar, but supply tariffs seem to vary hugely from place to place. Mains water cost is reasonable, as is the cost of rubbish removal. Fast internet access is ridiculously expensive. Staff costs are comparatively low, but you need to factor in the frequent holidays and religious and family ceremonies. Extras such as guest bonuses, or the common 'pay 13 months salary for 12 months work' lurk can add to costs. Eating out is cheap, and even cheaper when you discover that local warungs serve delicious, cheap food. High-end Western-style restaurants are expensive by Bali standards, but still considerably cheaper than at home.

Alcohol excise duties imposed by Jakarta in 2010 (350% to 500%), plus special taxes on top of that, were intended to be a cash cow, raising the cost of a bottle of scotch to about $90AUD and a bottle of very ordinary wine to $30-$50AUD. It also hit beer prices, but brewers have (for the time being) absorbed most of the increase - but have indicated the situation will not continue. One result is that alcohol aficionados buy far less now at those prices, reducing the government's tax take. The other result is a flourishing industry in stolen and bootleg liquor. The bootleg stuff often contains ethanol, and has already killed several hundred people, so add in the cost of a funeral to your Bali living expenses if you include village arak in your weekly spend.

Two variables are at work, of course. Living costs are lower, but the opportunities for a higher standard of living are greater, so, in common with a lot of expats, I opt for a comfortable life-style and pay a little more than I would otherwise be paying. It is possible to live very frugally and spend comparatively little, but few expats do.

## SHOPPING

*Is there anything in particular you haven't been able to find for sale in Bali, like household goods or food?*

Most stuff is available, although its quality is problematic in some cases. Many familiar brands are here, although their composition seems very different to the same brands back home. It really depends on your personal preferences.

Cadbury's chocolate is available here, but tastes very different because of the chemicals added here to prevent melting in hot climates. Mind you, for my palate, ever since they changed the Australian chocolate formula, even the stuff I buy at home tastes pretty ordinary.

Pantene shampoos and conditioners here seems to have a very different formula to those in Australia.

For those who rely on Quick-Eze as an antacid, bad luck - it's not available here.

I have never found a local can opener that works without disintegrating. My favourite deodorant is not available. Computer peripherals tend to be expensive. Tinned smoked oysters are virtually non-existent.

### *Do you have any favourite places for shopping?*

For day-today groceries and supplies, Bintang Supermarket is adequate, although its meat and fish section often smells like a week-old rubbish dumpster. For food such as meats and poultry, I prefer Casa Gourmet in Seminyak Square for its excellent quality and good price, although the range is limited. The range is better at Bali Deli, but prices tend to be high. Carrefour has a big range of food and the quality is good, but access on Jalan Sunset is problematic in heavy traffic and checkout queues are invariably long. Local markets are a great source of fresh fruit and vegetables at low prices.

### *INSURANCE*

### *One of the requirements for getting the retirement visa is showing proof of health insurance. Can you please tell me how you went about finding health cover?*

Stand-alone health and medical cover for Bali can cost an arm and leg - anywhere between $5,000 and $10,000AUD per annum. I discovered that purchasing a good world-wide extended travel insurance policy for 12 months or more (which is renewable online) also covers me for hospitalisation, medical emergencies and medical evacuation in the event of conditions requiring treatment in Australia or even Singapore.

The policy needs to be taken out in your home country BEFORE you leave for Bali, but after that, you can renew online each year or so. My policy is with World Nomads and costs me about $600 every 12 months. It covers me for world-wide travel except in the USA (and of course, my home country).

For medical cover when visiting home, I can merely reactivate my voluntarily-suspended Medibank Private cover should I ever need it.

### *SAFETY*

*Would you say Bali is a safe place to live? Have you ever felt unsafe?*

As regards terrorist attacks, I feel Bali is as safe as anywhere else where insane people are permitted to wander around with bombs. If I was going to worry about that kind of threat in Bali, I would spend most of my time hiding under the bed.

Safety on the roads is a different matter. Many of Bali's car and truck drivers, and the vast majority of Bali's motorbike riders are suicidal, spatially-challenged individuals who are completely bereft of road-craft skills or common sense. To stay safe on the roads requires a greatly-heightened awareness of risk factors. With care though, it is possible to go for hours without a near-miss or an actual collision.

Health safety also requires awareness of the risk factors that can cause serious disease here. Dengue fever and similar mosquito-borne health risks can be minimised by using repellent. Rabies is still prevalent here, necessitating care while around dogs. Venomous snakes can cause problems, even in urban areas, given that hospitals don't generally carry stocks of anti-venin.

Violent crime, though comparatively rare, does occur. Home invasions and burglaries do happen, bag-snatching happens and muggings, while infrequent, do occur. Good home security and being vigilant in high-risk situations can help minimise this.

Regardless of the above, I feel that with proper care, Bali is probably safer than Australia.

## MEDICAL AND HEALTH CARE

*One of the biggest concerns many people have about retiring in Bali is the perceived lack of quality health care. What has been your experience with medical care in Bali?*

Sophisticated medical care is not always available in Bali's local hospitals, who, while they do the best they can with the resources available, are sometimes not up to Western standards of equipment, training and funding. However, several hospitals have 'International Wings", which are better equipped, but of course more expensive.

There are also several medical centres intended for foreigners. These are usually very well-equipped and staffed, but have fairly young staff. In my experience, this can mean that some of the less-seasoned doctors tend to confirm their tentative diagnoses with a large number of pathology tests, which can bump up the cost of a consultation considerably. Fortunately a two-tier fee system exists, with KITAS holders getting a big discount. It is still expensive though. A second or third opinion is not a bad idea in Bali to minimise the chance of an expensive misdiagnosis.

There are also a number of good, Western-trained GPs who make house calls for about 600,000 rupiah.

Personally, if I had a medical emergency, or life-threatening injury, I would opt for medical evacuation to Australia or Singapore. Expect this to cost around $80,000 AUD if you have let your health insurance lapse, or about $100 AUD if you are covered.

## WEATHER

### Did you find it difficult to adjust to the warmer tropical climate?

Not at all. I arrived here at the beginning of a protracted cool season, so the adjustment was relatively painless. Now I have acclimatised to the extent that I don't sleep with the air-conditioner on if it is below 25C at night, I find that the pool is too cold to swim in between March and September, and I get cold riding the motorbike at night. Needless to say, nowadays a visit to Melbourne in winter is an unpleasant experience when one only owns tropical-style clothes.

## DAY TO DAY LIVING

### Do you ever feel "bored" living in Bali?

Never. I don't remember ever being bored in my life anyway, but Bali is so full of experiences and opportunities that there is more risk of stimulus overload than boredom.

*Did you join any formal clubs and did you find that was a good way to meet people?*

No. I'm not a joiner, nor do I enjoy 'organised' anything. I meet people from all walks of life here - locals, expats and visitors, and if we hit if off, that's nice; if not, that's fine too.

Friends however, say that clubs and sporting groups are a great way to meet new people. Each to their own.

## FAMILY AND FRIENDS

*Did you find it difficult leaving your family and friends behind in your home country?*

Yes, but I felt that any significant lifestyle shift would always incur some rough patches, so there was no point in delaying it. My family was supportive of the move as well, so the choice to move was not that difficult.

*Do you find it easy to keep in contact with them?*

Communication is easy, and Melbourne is only 5.5 hours flying time from Bali so it is not hard to reconnect when the need arises. Facebook, Skype, SMS, email and POTS (Plain Old Telephone System) make communication cheap and easy.

*How did you find making new friends in Bali, both foreign expats and Indonesian?*

I have made new friends here (both local and expat) through normal day-to-day activities. I also meet people online through my writing, and that sometimes translates into face-to-face meetings. I enjoy a fairly solitary life-style by both inclination and choice, and treasure the independence and freedom that gives me.

## TRANSPORT

*What is the main method you use to get around Bali?*

I bought a motorbike after a few months here, and it is my primary mode of transport in the local area. For extended trips to more remote parts of Bali, I hire a car and driver. Occasionally, I will use Bluebird taxis. If feeling uncharacteristically energetic, I walk.

### Did you get a local driver's license or use an international one?

I have Australian car and motorcycle licences, so I use a suitably endorsed International Driver's Permit here, which is valid for 12 months. I visit Australia once or twice a year, so it is no problem to renew it - it takes 10 minutes. A local licence is only valid for 12 months for foreigners anyway, so I see no point in getting one and then wasting most of a day each year getting it renewed at the local office here.

### Was it difficult to get used to driving in Bali?

It didn't take long, but the style of driving/riding here is *very* different, and needs extra care while acclimatising. In fact, it needs constant care just to stay alive and uninjured. If you like a challenge and enjoy high-risk activities, driving/riding in Bali is for you. Getting through intersections is basically a slow-motion game of bluff and passive-aggressive bullying. Give way to vehicles that are bigger, or who are about to hit you. Never lose your cool in the face of chaos and insanity, and you will be fine. Don't have an accident involving a local (even if it is totally their fault), because you, as a foreigner, will be expected to pay for all repairs, medical bills and compensation for any loss of earnings. Why? Because the 'victim' didn't invite you to Bali. If you hadn't come here, the accident would not have happened. Therefore, it is your fault. Can't fault the logic …

### Can you give any tips for buying a car/motorbike?

First, you must have a KITAS. Otherwise, you must buy the vehicle in the name of a local. Legally it becomes their vehicle; don't be surprised if one day they exercise their right of ownership under the law. For bikes, if you do have a KITAS, go to the dealer, show your KITAS, pay your money and go home. The bike will be delivered the same afternoon. Then you can look at it longingly for 2-3 weeks until the registration authorities get around to issuing your registration plates, which then allow you to actually ride it.

Locals just 'borrow' a set of plates until the real ones arrive, but I wouldn't recommend this for expats.

Buying a car can be more difficult. Dealers have been known to do the deal, then ask for more money for little extras like steering wheels and engines. *After* being paid, they may then inform you that the delivery date is 8 months hence. And when you finally do get the car, it will be a different model and colour to that ordered. OK, I exaggerate slightly for effect, but you get the picture. Caveat emptor. Ask others about their experiences. Employ the help of a reliable local.

## *HOUSING*

### *How did you go about finding housing in Bali?*

After trying a number of high-profile villa rental agencies and finding them somewhat lacking in either expertise or listening skills, and prone to showing me vastly over-priced properties, I gave up. I used one of the small property brokers instead. He listened to my requirements including location and price, asked me about my intended life-style in Bali and came up with a range of very well-suited properties to inspect. He scheduled all of the inspections, arranged lease documents, performed appropriate introductions with the property owners and saw the deal through to a satisfactory conclusion. The charge for his services was zero - the owner paid his commission.

### *Can you give any advice for finding housing to future expats?*

View as wide a selection of properties as you can. Choose a location that not only suits, but fits in with your day-today shopping needs, security considerations and transport availability. Check the cost of utilities - electricity supply costs in particular vary widely. Check that the electricity supply available to the property is adequate - some properties have such an inadequate supply that running two air-conditioners and a pool pump will trip the breakers. Increasing the supply limit can take months if not years. Check water costs (either well-water or mains), rubbish removal costs and any 'donations' that might be expected by your local banjar to ensure that things run smoothly. Check whether a phone line is connected - if not, it might take up to a year for a connection to be made. Check whether a backup generator is installed - power outages are frequent in Bali.

Check for the availability of a reasonable internet service. If there is a phone line, check that it good enough to handle ADSL, otherwise you will be stuck with dial-up, which in Bali means it is s - l - o - w. If there is no phone line, check that a wireless signal is available in your area.

### STAFF

***One of the requirements of getting the retirement visa is that you agree to employ someone to help take care of your house, how did you go about finding staff?***

Initially, my staff were previous employees of the outgoing villa tenant. Additional or replacement staff were sourced through personal recommendations.

***Can you give any tips or advice for finding household staff in Bali?***

Agencies are available who can supply staff, but you may find that you are up for a hefty commission.

Personal recommendations from employers can be another good source, but check the one who is doing the recommending too, so you get an idea of what they regard as 'good' qualities. Asking for recommendations from your local banjar is a good PR move, and will be more likely to get you someone from the local area who will get to work on time.

I always employ new staff on a 1-month trial period, followed by a 3 month probationary period. I also make it very clear at the outset what transgressions (such as stealing) will result in instant dismissal.

Unless you speak Bahasa, it is a good idea to get someone who speaks English. Miscommunication due to cultural factors is frequent enough; there is no point in compounding it further with a language barrier.

Expect that your Balinese staff will frequently take time off for a huge variety of ceremonies, sometimes with very little notice. Expect that Javanese staff who are Muslims will often require time off for prayer and for various holy days, including an expectation of 1-2 weeks off towards the end of the fasting month of Ramadan, plus a hefty holiday bonus.

Be careful when giving bonuses to explain what they are for. Staff given a one-off bonus on a payday sometimes get upset when the same bonus doesn't materialise the following month, believing that they have done something wrong to have it 'taken away' from them.

## INTERNET

### What has been your experience using the internet in Bali?

I started with a landline phone-based ADSL broadband service feeding a modem and wi-fi. This worked adequately, but was slow and clunky compared to some Western countries. It cost around 350,000 per month and was added to the phone bill.

After moving to a new villa without a landline, I had to use USB stick modem from Indosat that cost 200,000 per month and provided barely adequate service for a few months before my local tower became completely overloaded with subscribers and the service became unuseable. As the provider continued to promote and sell the subscriber service despite its infrastructure being a full capacity, the drop-outs and very slow speed became unbearable and I switched providers.

I am now with CBN, who installed a high-gain antenna on the roof connected to a modem and wi-fi set-up which gives me high-speed broadband of consistently high quality. The downside is, it costs me 700,000 per month.

As an alternative, cheap internet cafes abound here, as does free wi-fi in a number of restaurants.

## CONCLUSION

### How different do you think your life would have been if you had decided to retire in your own country?

I would have been stuck with a much lower standard of living and would have burned through my cash reserves much faster. I would have had to put up with an over-regulated social environment with ludicrous rules emanating relentlessly from all tiers of government, and a winter climate which is not to my liking.

Unlike Bali, which is close to a main Asian travel hub, Australia is so far from everywhere that my opportunities for cheap travel would have been severely limited.

In fact, I probably would have needed to work for another 8 years before even contemplating retirement if I had decided to stay in Australia.

***Did you make any kind of backup plan if things didn't go well after moving to Bali?***

Malaysia, Thailand and Vietnam were all on the radar if my master plan of writing while living a life of sloth and gluttony in Bali failed to come to fruition. They still are.

***If you had to do it all again would you do anything different?***

Not a thing.

***Could you just give one or two pieces of advice for anyone who might be considering retiring in Bali?***

Do your homework prior to coming here, so that you are aware that this is a foreign country and that things are done here VERY differently. Remember at all times that you are a guest in this country. Adjust your attitude accordingly.

Remember that this is a civil jurisdiction, not one operating under Common Law. This means that anything you hear about the result of any court case does NOT set a legal precedent.

Caveat emptor. Plausible sob-stories abound here and scams are rife. Do not assume that expats are any more or less trustworthy than the locals. If a deal or offer here  seems too good to be true, it probably is. Don't lend money. You are highly unlikely ever to see it again. Don't sell anything without getting paid first.

Oh, and be aware that your KITAS renewal each year can take anywhere between 1 month and 4 months. Mine took over 2 months for each renewal so far. During this time, the authorities retain your passport, which means you can not travel anywhere, not even to other Indonesian destinations, because your passport is demanded almost everywhere as preferred ID.

## The Importance of Making Local Friends in Bali

The following is an interview with Shane from Australia. You can read more about her adventures in Bali on her blog: http://baliquest.wordpress.com

*Can you please start by telling me how you became interested in Bali?*

In 2008 we came to Bali on holiday with a friend. We spent a few days on the beach in the south before heading up to Ubud which is where we became enchanted with Bali.

*There are several different countries that offer retirement visa programs, can you tell me, what made you decide on Bali?*

As a professional speaker Bob travelled the world and we've stayed at countless beaches that mostly run together in my mind but Ubud was unique. The weather, the people with their winning smiles and kind natures, and that intangible quality of serenity made the place memorable.

In 2010 we started talking about moving overseas from Australia and made a reconnaissance trip in April to see if it still felt magical. It did and we didn't waste any time. In June we moved to Bali.

*Did you spend much time looking at other possible retirement destinations?*

Not really. We briefly considered Fiji because we have spent a lot of time there and know it well but it didn't beckon like Bali did.

*Most people who live in Bali say that it is a very different experience than just coming for holiday. What has been your experience and what do you think are the main differences?*

Living in Bali as opposed to visiting is sort of like being married as opposed to a committed relationship. It's hard to say why it is different but it is. We relaxed because we weren't trying to squeeze all the experiences into a few days. We made firm friendships with people who know we won't be gone in a week or two. We scouted out the best grocery store as opposed to the best restaurants although we are still interested in the good places to eat. We are more interested in the welfare of the island and its people than we would be as tourists. Bali has that quality of being our "home". We look out at the world rather than looking in at Bali.

*VISAS*

*Can you please explain how you went about applying for the retirement visa?*

On our reconnaissance trip we were driving by a visa agent and simply went in to begin the application process.

*There are many different agents offering visa services, how did you go about selecting your agent?*

When we originally applied for our visa we simply stopped at one that was convenient and visible. However, when we renewed our visa a year later we found a man who was recommended to us by someone on the BaliPod.com website. He was less expensive and provided excellent service.

*Knowing about the process now, would you do anything differently?*

Not really, other than using a different agent as previously described.

*MAKING THE MOVE*

*Can you describe how you shipped your personal belongings to Bali? How was the experience?*

We had a large shipment and used Movements International. The move from Australia seemed to go well, but went downhill in Indonesia. We paid an extra AU$2,000 to get our shipment through customs. The Balinese agent for Movements International was a glorified name for some roughshod cowboys who broke or damaged some of our furniture in their rough handling.

*Can you give any advice to people who are looking to move everything they own to Bali?*

Having read the advice given in the BaliPod forum we knew we should be judicious in deciding what to bring. We probably either sold or gave away 70% of our stuff and we're glad we did. The important things to bring are those with which there is an emotional attachment.

*Do you remember before you moved to Bali that you had any big concerns or worries?*

We tend to be impulsive and optimistic by nature and didn't really have any serious concerns about our move. Mostly we just felt excited.

## CULTURE

*Did you study much about Balinese culture before you came here?*

Not too much. From the time we decided to move until the move was made we only had two months and that time was spent finalizing things in Australia and preparing for the move to Bali.

*If so, do you have any advice for people to learn more about Balinese culture?*

There are some great books about the Balinese people and the Balinese culture. We've found it much easier to settle into Bali knowing more about the habits, culture, and people. Learning the Indonesian language is also a huge help.

## GOVERNMENT

*When I did a survey of people who were considering retiring in Bali, "government stability" or instability was a common concern for many people. What are your feelings and experience on this?*

Especially now that the U.S. is experiencing an alarming economic downturn we're glad to be in an Asian country that may withstand an economic downturn better than some countries. Perhaps we're too complacent but we feel as though we're living in one of the better places on the planet for political and economic instability.

*Another concern people had about moving to Bali is corruption in the government and police. What has been your experience and do you think it is something for people who are thinking to retire in Bali, need to be concerned about?*

It seems that the people who tend to feel the most like victims are the ones who talk the most about corruption. In most situations paying money under the table is a choice, not a necessity. We have not been stopped by the police but paying money can hurry things along in many instances. It hasn't been a problem in our experience.

## COST OF LIVING

*How do you find the cost of living in Bali and how does it compare with your home country?*

We find the cost of living to be far less than the cost of living in Australia. Eating in expensive western restaurants is a choice but there is an abundance of restaurants where is cost is unbelievably low. Many other costs are also low such as groceries, petrol, household staff, services, etc.

*Bali has long been considered a cheap place for a holiday or to live. Do you think that this is still the case?*

Yes, Bali still is less expensive for a holiday or for living than many western countries.

## SHOPPING

***Is there anything in particular haven't been able to find for sale in Bali, like household goods or food?***

There are a few things we haven't found in Bali but nothing that really matters. Actually we've found many food items from the U.S. are available in Bali that weren't available in Australia.

***Do you have any favorite places for shopping?***

For groceries we shop at Delta Dewata and Bintang in Ubud. I also occasionally make a trip to Hardy's Gourmet in Sanur.

## INSURANCE

***One of the requirements for getting the retirement visa is showing proof of health insurance. Can you please tell me how you went about finding health cover?***

I chose Health Care International by comparing prices on the internet but health care insurance in Bali is far too expensive and I'm looking now for a better option.

## SAFETY

***Would you say Bali is a safe place to live? Have you ever felt unsafe?***

I've never felt unsafe in Bali for a single minute.

## MEDICAL AND HEALTH CARE

*One of the biggest concerns many people have about retiring in Bali is the perceived lack of quality health care. What has been your experience with medical care in Bali?*

We would agree with the perception that medical care in Bali is of a much lower standard than we ever experienced in the U.S. or in Australia. Thankfully we haven't had any serious or lifethreatening illnesses in Bali and wouldn't want to be in Bali hoping for any high-standard medical care.

## WEATHER

*Did you find it difficult to adjust to the warmer tropical climate?*

We love the weather and haven't found it to be as hot as we expected but we're living in an area with almost constant cooling breezes.

## DAY TO DAY LIVING

*Do you ever feel "bored" living in Bali?*

Bored? In Bali? Never. We've hardly scratched the surface of things we can do here.

*Did you join any formal clubs and did you find that was a good way to meet people?*

Neither of us has felt drawn to search out western friends. We have some western friends and a few Balinese friends. I don't believe it is difficult at all to make friends in Bali. We have found the expats and the Balinese to be very willing to extend the hand of friendship.

## FAMILY AND FRIENDS

*Did you find it difficult leaving your family and friends behind in your home country?*

Yes. Very difficult. We've been very fortunate to have family and friends come to Bali to visit but leaving them was the only difficult part of our move.

*Do you find it easy to keep in contact with them?*

Thank heavens for the internet and reasonably priced flights, not to mention the lure of Bali.

*How did you find making new friends in Bali, both foreign expats and Indonesian?*

We haven't spent any time trying to make friends. It has just happened naturally over time and we feel very fortunate to have wonderful, kind, caring, and interesting Balinese and expat friends.

## TRANSPORT

*What is the main method you use to get around Bali?*

I drive a car and my husband drives a motorbike. Now that we're used to the Balinese road customs and conditions we aren't having any trouble getting around the island.

*Did you get a local driver's license or use an international one?*

We both now have local driver's licenses.

*Was it difficult to get used to driving in Bali?*

Perhaps it was scary rather than difficult. The best advice we received was "go slow and watch out for others".

## HOUSING

*How did you go about finding housing in Bali?*

Having a Balinese friend was invaluable in finding a rental house to live in while we built our house. His trusted guidance made all the difference in having a well-built house and an easy, pleasant building experience.

*Can you get any advice for finding housing to future expats?*

The best advice we could give would be to rent while making a decision about which area to live in and to listen to the advice of a Balinese friend. Some areas are definitely not friendly to foreigners. Some are very welcoming. As expats it is difficult to know the difference. It is important to talk to the village leader.

*What made you want to build a house in Bali and how was the experience?*

We wanted to build for a couple of reasons. One, we wanted to build on a specific block of land and two, we wanted to build a particular style of house. The experience couldn't have been easier. We've built many houses over the years and this was probably the easiest. We had a great builder and wonderful sub-contractors. Our Balinese friend acted as a manager for the complete job and that made all the difference. He and my husband were at the site, all day every day.

## STAFF

*One of the requirements of getting the retirement visa is that you agree to employ someone to help take care of your house, how did you go about finding staff?*

We hired someone we already knew. We have only one staff person, a man. He does most of the interior cleaning. He also handles the pond maintenance, the pool maintenance and some of the gardening. He is also willing to run errands or do any shopping we ask him to do. I do the washing. The ironging is done by a local laundry. We also have a gardener come in occasionally to do some planting or maintenance of the garden or pond plants.

*Can you give any tips or advice for finding household staff in Bali?*

Finding someone was never an issue. We had a number of people come to us asking for a job. We had known the man we hired for a year and completely trust him. Trust is probably the most important issue so it's best to take things slowly. It is also very useful to make friends in the community.

## INTERNET

### What has been your experience using the internet in Bali?

Our experience has been frustrating. Our Telkomsel service is painfully slow. We do not live in an area where land lines are available. Improving our internet service is something we're presently working on.

## CONCLUSION

### How different do you think your life would have been if you had decided to retire in your own country?

We do not believe it would have been nearly as interesting or as pleasant. Our money goes much further in Bali than it would in Australia.

### Did you make any kind of backup plan if things didn't go well after moving to Bali?

We do not have a backup plan but that's just our nature. A backup plan is probably an excellent idea.

### If you had to do it all again would you do anything different?

We would not have done anything differently but we've also been very lucky in our Bali experience.

### Could you just give one or two pieces of advice for anyone who might be considering retiring in Bali?

My advice would be to come to Bali with an open mind and a sense of adventure. Living in Bali is different from anywhere else but it is different in a good way. The Balinese are lovely, accepting people. The other bit of advice I would strongly give is to make some Balinese friends and let them guide you from their experience.

## *Getting involved with community groups*

The following is an interview I did with Ron from Australia. Ron has been living in Bali for the past few years on the retirement visa and is an active member in the Lovina Rotary Club (http://www.rotary-bali-lovina.org)

**Can you please start by telling me how you became interested in Bali?**

I came first as a tourist in about 1988 and kept coming back many times since. I always came to Lovina.

**There are several different countries that offer retirement visa programs; can you tell me what made you decide on Bali?**

Mainly because my partner is Indonesian and traveling to visit family is much easier.

**Did you consider staying anywhere else in Indonesia?**

I guess we could have considered Sulawesi where my partner is from, but I felt more comfortable staying somewhere with more western influence that can is found in Bali.

**Most people who live in Bali say it is a very different experience than just coming for holiday. What has been your experience and what do you think are the main differences.**

It is not hugely different, but it is different in the way that you have to interact a bit more with the local bureacracy just to get your electricity, water. So you spend more time making sure you have everything that you need, if you are building, you would be interacting with building supply places and so on. You are interacting with people on a different level.

<u>Visas</u>

*Can you please explain how you went about applying for the retirement visa?*

It was very easy. I just used an agent here. I had a social visa for the first six months. The agent here set it up.

*There are many different agents offering visa services, how did you go about selecting your agent?*

Just by talking to other people.

<u>Making the move</u>

*Can you describe how you shipped your personal belongings to Bali? How was the experience?*

We found a freight company in Sydney to just ship it, but they were not going to deliver it to Bali. So they were just going to ship it and then it was going to arrive in Denpasar and then we would be contacted. We just found an agent at the airport who was there at the time and we used her and she helped us find a truck. It looked as though it was going to rain and the truck didn't have a tarp (cover) so she had to send someone out on a motorbike to get one.

So just practicalities. The truck driver had never been to Singaraja so he wanted us to drive in front and lead them. This was soon after we had arrived and I was still a bit nervous driving. Apart from taking them down a street in Singaraja, which trucks aren't allowed to go down, everything went okay.

**I recently did a survey with people interested in retiring to Bali and one of concerns a few people had was government stability. What are**

**your feelings or experience with this?**

I started doing some work on a consultancy basis in Jakarta in 1998, just after some riots and was working with some Australians who had to evacuate and before that happened they would have said there was no problem in Indonesia. The evacuation took them totally by surprise. The situation changed from being stable to chaotic in a very quick time. So things like that can happen, but there is no sign of that at present. That might be a once in 50 years event.

**Another concern some people have about moving to Bali is the corruption in the government and the police. What has been your experience, and do you think it is something that people need to be concerned about?**

No, I don't think it is something you need to be concerned about. It doesn't affect you directly if you are just living here. People who are conducting business here and trying to get building permits and things like that are more likely to experience this. With regard to people who just live here, for most of their interactions they tend to use an agent and any incentive payments that are passed off, you don't see directly and you don't have to worry about it.

**How do you find the cost of living in Bali and how does it compare with your home country?**

Mostly it is cheaper, but some things are more expensive. Electricity in a big house is not cheaper. Internet is more expensive, but other than that, most things are cheaper. If I had stayed in Australia as a retired person, I would have gotten all of the benefits that retirees get in Australia.

**So electricity is more expensive than what it is in Australia?**

A similar price, maybe a little bit more. You pay a lot more with a big house. For a small house, you can pay the rent, the electricity, the Indovision, the water and the internet all for less than the electricity on a big house.

**Is there anything in particular that you haven't been able to find for**

**sale in Bali, like household goods or any kind of food?**

Sometimes there is a bit of a challenge to find things, but you eventually find them. The thing we miss the most is a higher selection of wines at affordable prices than what you can find in Australia. So I love going back there for wine shopping.

**Do you have any favorite places to go shopping?**

For computers we go to the Remo Trade Center. When we are down south, we go to Lotte Mart, which was Makro.

**One of the requirements for getting the retirement visa is showing proof of health insurance, can you tell me how you went about finding health coverage?**

For the first three years, they never even asked about that. The agent always made sure I had liability insurance, but never mentioned health insurance, until this year. This year it just so happened that I had been worrying enough about health insurance that I decided to get some. So it wasn't a big issue.

**What is the liability insurance?**

It covers all sorts of things, like if someone dove into your pool and broke their neck, but I am not exactly sure. I think it is just to make sure that you aren't going to be an expense to the community.

**Would you say Bali is a safe place to live, and have you ever felt unsafe?**

Yes, it's a safe place to live. It's not unsafe and doesn't give a feel like you might get mugged. The biggest risks are probably health risks.

**A concern for many people is health care, what has been your experience so far with medical care in Bali?**

For the hospitals in the north, if you need a few stitches or something it's fine, but if you have something where the diagnosis is a bit more difficult, I don't have much faith in them. In the south at hospitals like BIMC, I have more faith in their ability to diagnose, and I think they would also advise you when you need to seek treatment outside of Bali.

**Did you find it difficult to adjust to the warmer, tropical climate?**

No.

**Do you ever feel bored living in Bali?**

I don't think so.

**Did you join any formal clubs and did you find it was a good way to meet people?**

For the first couple of years I didn't, then I joined the local Rotary Club and that is useful getting involved in some group activities.

**What kind of activities does Rotary get involved in?**

The club here has an environmental project mainly to do with: waste management, beach clean ups, doing things with schools, literacy programs, helping local libraries and HIV awareness programs.

**Did you find it difficult to leave your friends and family behind in your home country?**

Not really. Some of them have come to Bali and it's not so difficult to go back.

**How did you find making friends with other people, locals and expats?**

It's very easy to meet people and start talking, and I've probably created friendships here with people that I might not have back in Australia. Here you are more open to spending time with people that have different interests. My Indonesian is quite poor so the locals I am friends with speak some English.

**What is the main method of transport you use to get around Bali?**

136

A car... I have thought about motorbikes, but haven't tried that yet. When you're driving around, you see people falling off motorbikes and it makes you think, "Oh, God."

**Did you get a local license or did you use an international one?**

For the first 12 months I had an international one and then a local license.

**Was that easy to get here?**

Yes, it's easy to get. That's one of the places where you need a little bit of corruption and you pay more than a local would.

**Was it difficult to get used to driving around?**

It does take a little bit of adjusting. The adjustment was mainly just to go slow and realize there is no such thing as having a right of way.

**How did you go about finding housing in Bali?**

We mainly looked at development companies here. Their prices are moderately high, but they deliver without much trouble.

**Can you give any advice for people looking to find housing?**

My inclination if I was doing it again would be to rent for longer first and give more consideration to buy an established house. However, when you have two people involved, you have different views and if one partner wants to create a new home and to do it fairly quickly, then the slower approach of renting and looking around, just won't work.

**Why do you say it is better to rent for longer?**

The reason to rent would be, to get a bit more acclimatized and to get a stronger feeling if you want to be by the beach or in the hills, or in the middle of a town. The reason for buying an existing house is that there are basically a number of quite good ones available. You have to ask yourself, why go to the trouble and angst, worrying if it will turn out as the building company promised.

**One of the requirements of getting the retirement visa is that you agree to employ someone to take care of your house. How did you go about finding staff?**

In the beginning, the project company we were using, had a local lady which they called the "helpdesk". She helps finding housekeepers and the guy we got as security had been working for the building company as security staff up until the house was finished and we decided to keep employing him to watch our house.

**I believe you brought your dog here before the ban on bringing dogs into Bali, due to rabies outbreak; can you tell me how that went?**

It was quite easy, but quite expensive. The dog cost more for an airfare, if you bundle in the cost of agents at each end and with the airfare, the dog's travel costs were more than us.

**Were you able to at that time, bring your dogs straight to Bali?**

Yes, straight to Bali. Strictly should have stayed in quarantine, but presumably if you pay enough money to the right people....

**What has been your experience with the internet in Bali?**

You pay more and you get much worse, but in the end nevertheless it works. You don't use YouTube much because it is so slow, but everything else more or less works.

**How different do you think your life would have been if you had of decided to retire in your own country?**

It would be quite different. You would do some of the same things, like try and find clubs and things. In other situations you are trying to adjust your expenses to your retirement income, which is a whole lot less than a working income, but the decisions that you make in Bali are quite different to the ones you would make in Australia. So as time goes by the lifestyle that develops, must become quite different.

**Did you make a backup plan, if things in Bali didn't work out as you expected?**

We did think about that. We thought—why not plan for five years initially and then reassess.

**If you had to do it all again, is there anything you would have done differently?**

One spectacular bad decision we made was buying a dishwasher, which has never really worked. It looks like an expensive paper weight.

**Finally, can you give one or two pieces of advice for anyone who might be thinking about retiring in Bali?**

I would suggest putting off decisions longer, if you can, because your attitude to different things will change after living in Bali for a while. Things that you might have thought in the beginning fade away and don't seem very important.

# Final thoughts on retiring to Bali

Making any kind of move can be a stressful time. If you think back to the last time you moved house, you can start to imagine how much more stressful an international move will be. If you are moving with your spouse, moving overseas can place stress on the relationship.

You really need to maintain a good sense of humor while living in Bali. If you start stressing about small things, you could become more stressed out than if you stayed at home. Life in Bali should be as peaceful and idyllic as you imagined it to be. You may need to learn to be a more patient person. In Indonesian, 'besok' literally means tomorrow; however, you will start to realize that can also mean next week, next month or in the worst case next year!

Don't just move to Bali because you think it will be a cheap place to live. Certainly, that can be a positive aspect, but it shouldn't be the only reason why you want to retire in Bali. In fact, while the cost of living might be cheaper than the country you are from, you don't get any of the health or other government benefits you might get in your home country, such as subsidized medicine and health care.

Get involved in community groups once you have settled in. Not only are they a good place to make new friends, they can help to provide invaluable information and advice about your new home.

Start studying Indonesian before you leave and continue your studies after you arrive. You will have a much more rewarding experience and being able to speak the languge will open so many more doors and opportunities to mix with people who don't speak English.

Remember the phases that you will inevitably go through when you move to Bali. After the initial 'honeymoon' period, experiencing a major set back that might make you wonder if you made the right decision and finally acceptance. If you hit a low point during your stay, I would suggest to do a bit of travel, either to a different part of Bali or even somewhere else in Indonesia. Stay in a nice place and I am sure it will help to make you realize whether you made the right move or not.

If you are an introverted or shy person, you need to learn to be a little outgoing. Initially at least you will need to be the one to invite people out somewhere or for a meal, or to your house. If someone invites you out somewhere, do your best to accept the invitation. When you were living in your home country, you may have only made friends with certain kinds of people. In Bali, you will need to be a little more open. One of the good things about living in Bali, is the wide variety of people you can meet, all from different countries, backgrounds and interests.

Try to make friends with people who have a positive outlook on life and actually enjoy living in Bali. You would be surprised at the number of people who live in Bali, who are quite negative about the place. It is common for expats when they get together to make complaints about problems in Bali. I think occassionally this is healthy, especially if people are also sharing their positive experiences. The only problem is people who are continually negative. Spending too much time with these kinds of people will eventually affect your own outlook of life in Bali.

Bali has so much to offer as a tourist destinaiton and a place to spend retirement, but like anywhere in the world, you will only get back what you give. Swimming in your villa pool everyday and not getting out and meeting new people and having new experiences will get old very quickly. Get out and explore: try different food, practice the language, meet new people, drive to a different part of the island or attend a ceremony. Certainly Bali has it's problems and it's not going to be paradise for everyone, but at least (in my humble opinion), it is pretty darn close.

# Further reading

Living in Indonesia, A Site for Expatriates (www.expat.or.id) – An excellent website that covers all aspects of living in Indonesia, with a very busy forum.

Learning Indonesian (www.learningindonesian.com) – A fantastic website to help you learn Indonesian with free and paid downloadable guides and podcasts.

Where to Retire (www.bestplacestoretire.com) - An American print magazine aimed at Americans who are looking to move within the United States or overseas for their retirement.

Bali Discovery (www.balidiscovery.com) – Travel booking website with an excellent weekly email newsletter, covering all of the latest news and events in Bali.

The Bali Times (www.thebalitimes.com) – Online version of Bali's largest English language newspaper.

# Appendix A - Sample sponsor letter

The following is a sample sponsor letter which is required for the Social Visa (social budaya). Simply copy and paste the text into a new document and edit it so it reflects yours and your sponsor's details. Make sure you get your sponsor to sign the letter.

Br ADD YOUR SPONSOR'S BANJAR
Desa ADD YOUR SPONSOR'S DESA
Bali
Indonesia

ADD THE INDONESIAN EMBASSY OR CONSULATE'S ADDRESS TO WHICH YOU WILL BE APPLYING, FOR EXAMPLE

Kepada Yth
Bapak Pimpinan Imigrasi
Kedutaan Besar Republik Indonesia
Di Singapura

21 December 2011 ADD CURRENT DATE

Dengan Hormat

Yang bertanda tangan dibawah ini saya

Nama : ADD YOUR SPONSOR'S NAME
Umur : ADD YOUR SPONSOR'S AGE (Kelahiran: ADD YOUR SPONSOR'S PLACE & DATE OF BIRTH)
Alamat : ADD YOUR SPONSOR'S ADDRESS
Pekerjaan : ADD YOUR SPONSOR'S OCCUPATION
Nomor KTP : ADD YOUR SPONSOR'S KTP NUMBER

Dengan ini menyatakan bahwa,

Nama : ADD YOUR NAME
Kebangsaan : ADD YOUR NAME NATIONALITY
Normor paspor : ADD YOUR PASSPORT NUMBER
Tempat – Tgl lahir : ADD YOUR DATE & PLACE OF BIRTH AS IN YOUR PASSPORT
Pekerjaan : ADD YOUR YOUR PROFESSION

Adalah kenalan saya yang akan ke Indonesia untuk mengadakan kunjungan kepada keluarga saya.

ADD YOUR NAME AS IT APPEARS IN YOUR PASSPORT, sejak lama kenal sebagai orang yang berkelakuan baik dan tidak pernah tersangkut urusan Kepolisian Republik Indonesia. Selama kunjungannya kepada saya, ia akan menjadi tanggung jawab dan dibawah pengawasan saya.

Demikian pernyataan ini saya buat dengan sejujur-jujurnya, agar menjadi perhatian Bapak seperlunya.

Untuk itu saya mengucapkan banyak terima kasih.

Hormat saya

ADD YOUR SPONSOR'S NAME & SIGNATURE
Sponsor

# Appendix B – Interviews with visa consulting companies

## Bali Mode

Address: Jl.Sriwijaya No. 7 Legian - Kuta
Telephone: 0361-765162
Fax : 0361-763562
E-Mail: balimode@hotmail.com
Website: balimode-biz.com

**Can you give an overview of how to qualify for the retirement visa?**

A retirement visa is a visa valid for five years, allowing foreigners to be semi resident for the country of Indonesia which need to be renewed every year with the purpose of retired visit.

You are not allowed to work or having any engaged of company or employment under this visa.

**What documents are necessary for getting the retirement visa?**

Requirements for applying for the visa:

- Minimum 55 years old
- Copy pages of at least 18 months validity passport
- Copy of marriage certificate (for couple)
- Copy of bank statement for living accommodation
- Copy of health insurance
- Statement to declare employment of Indonesian maid servant/housekeeper
- Photograph size 4x6 : 6 pcs
- Company sponsorship (our company will be your sponsor)

**Should people apply for their visa in their home country or in Bali?**

You need to go to Indonesian Embassy overseas or at your home country.

We will have submit your documents to our head immigration in Jakarta to get a recommendation letter of approval " Calling Visa" , once they approved you, they will issue a notification for you to go to your nominated Indonesian Embassy to apply for visa.

We will need around 10 -15 working days to proceed it at the head immigration.

**How long does the whole visa application process take?**

There are two procedures time processing to get the visa :

First is getting approval from the head immigration (10-15 working days); once they approve you, you need to go to embassy to apply for a visa.

For the visa application processing time will need to find out at the embassy overseas; however, they will normally take 5-7 working days.

Second, once you have the visa and entering the country, we will need your passport to be submitted to local immigration office to proceed KITAS (semi permanent card).

It will take around 2-3 weeks working days.

The whole processing time is about 2 months, before and after.

**If someone comes to Indonesia on a social visa and then they apply for the retirement visa, do they need to exit the country to pick up their visa at an Indonesian embassy overseas, like in Singapore? Or can everything be done in Indonesia?**

A new kind of visa must be obtained at the Indonesian Embassy.

A social visa is different from a retirement visa, so yes, you have to leave the country of Indonesia and go to an Indonesian Embassy overseas ( e.g. Singapore).

**Do you need a sponsor and how should people go about finding a sponsor?**

Yes, we do provide sponsorship.

**What happens if one partner is over 55 for example and qualifies for the visa and their partner is say 45 years old. What can they do about this?**

They can be attached (retired visa) by family visa for family reunion—they will be charged as well.

**Do people who retire in Bali have to pay tax in Indonesia on their pension?**

They will not need to pay tax; however, they will need to do report monthly or annually for their pension to the Tax Department - and in connection with this the Tax Dept. will issue a tax personal card ( NPWP) with one of its function is for fiscal clearance.

if you are not registered, you have to pay for fiscal tax rp 2.500.000 every time leaving the country.

**Should people who want to retire in Bali get an NPWP?**

See above.

**How can people move their possessions to Bali? Can you help with that?**

A mover company will be needed to handle this.

**Can you tell me how much the retirement visa costs for one applicant?**

Retirement visa costs for each applicant is Rp 6.500.000

Extra costs will charge for ;

Visa Application at the embassy

Exit Permit ( for Kitas holder, there will need an exit permit to leave the country, the length of exit permit validity will depends on your needs ).

- ⅄ Multiple Exit Reentry Permit valid for 11 months
- ⅄ Multiple Exit Reentry Permit valid for 6 months
- ⅄ Single Exit Reentry Permit valid for 3 months
- ⅄ Emergency Exit Reentry Permit valid for 30 days

Fiscal Fee
Airport Tax
Mutasion

**How much is the cost for renewal?**

**What is the maximum length of time someone can stay on a retirement visa in Indonesia?**

Please see above.

**Can you please give a brief introduction to your company and tell us about what services you provide to retired expats? How does your company differ from the many other visa agencies in Bali?**

Please see our website for more information about our company.

# KenKen Bali

Address: Jl. Dewi Sri, Pert. Suryamas No. 2, Legian, Kuta

Telephone: 0361-8778475

Website: http://www.kenkenbali.com

*Can you give an overview of how to qualify for the retirement visa? What documents are necessary for getting the retirement visa?*

A retirement visa is given to a foreigner who is 55 years old or older when they apply.

The documents needed to support the application include:

Copy full pages passport, copy of Marriage Certificate for couple and 2 pcs photograph size 4cm X 6cm. To have retirements visa the applicants need a sponsor who complete with the license to sponsoring retirements.

How to process:

After we have all documents from the applicant and sponsor then we will apply to Directorate General Immigration in Jakarta to get a TELEX VISA; this process will take three weeks. After we get the telex visa from Jakarta then we will send it to the applicant by email and they will bring the telex visa to the Indonesian Embassy overseas (but before they apply the applicant should decide which Indonesian Embassy will they apply at) this process will take around three days and some fees will be charged by the embassy. After we get the visa and the applicant arrives in Bali the immigration will give an admission stamp for temporary stay for seven

seven days during which time the applicant needs to report their arrival to the immigration office in Bali to process KITAS (Semi Permanent Residence) and police registration. Two weeks after reporting the applicant will get a schedule to sign and interview with immigration and one week after they will get a Kitas from immigration.

**Should people apply for their visa in their home country or in Bali?**

People can apply for the visa from their country, but if the applicant was in Bali then they could apply from Bali too as long there was an agent who would process the recommendation from Directorate General Immigration in Jakarta as TELEX VISA.

**How long does the whole visa application process take?**

As per our explanation above, the total time needed to process KITAS is six weeks (three weeks to process Telex Visa and three weeks to process Kitas).

**If someone comes to Indonesia on a social visa and then they apply for the retirement visa, do they need to exit the country to pick up their visa at an Indonesian embassy overseas, like in Singapore? Or can everything be done in Indonesia?**

If at the beginning they come to Indonesia with a Social Visa and then they apply for the retirement visa from Indonesia they should leave Indonesia again to take the visa after the telex visa ready, like in Singapore or other country.

**Do you need a sponsor and how should people go about finding a sponsor?**

Yes, to apply for a retirement visa the applicant needs a sponsor which our company can provide.

**Can you tell me how much the retirement visa costs for one applicant?**

The cost to have a Retirements Visa is IDR.7.000.000., this cost including process: Sponsorship, Telex Visa, Kitas, Blue Book (control book from immigration) and Police registration from police center in Jakarta and District in Bali.

**How much is the cost for renewal?**

The cost to renew every year is IDR.6.500.000.

**What happens if one partner is over 55 for example and qualifies for the visa and their partner is say 45 years old. What can they do about this?**

If the one partner is less than 45 years old, as long they are legally married, we can apply for Family Visa as Kitas Holder (this is for the wife and children only). The cost for apply this Visa is the same to process retirement visa as above.

**Do people who retire in Bali have to pay tax in Indonesia on their pension?**

For foreigners who stay more than 180 days without leaving, they must pay income tax in Indonesia.

**Should people who want to retire in Bali get an NPWP?**

Yes, they must to have personal tax number (NPWP) because for Kitas holder same like half Indonesia so if they leave Indonesia should pay Fiscal tax amount Idr.2.500.000., if they have personal tax number so they will no charge for fiscal at the airport.

### What is the maximum length of time someone can stay on a retirement visa in Indonesia?

Retirees can stay for 5 years in Indonesia without leaving. If they need to leave they must apply for an **Exit Permit Re-Entry** and there are 4 kinds of exit permits for re-entry: a Single Exit Re-entry permit which is valid for 3 months and costs Idr.700.000, a Multiplr Exit Re-entry permit for 6 months with the cost Idr.1.100.000, a Multiple Exit Re-entry permit for 1 year with the cost Idr. 1.700.000, and an Exit Permit Only with the cost Idr.500.000.

### How can people move their possessions to Bali? Can you help with that?

For foreigners, if they want to move their possession to Bali they can send their goods through a forwarding company such as PERSONAL EFFECT, but they must be a kitas holder first. This personal import can be used one time only. As a suggestion, before you send goods it's better to prepare the cargo agent in Bali for clearance in Custom in Indonesia. We can help with this.

### Can you please give a brief introduction to your company and tell us about what services you provide to retired expats

Our Company is KENKEN BALI, and more details can be found on our website www.kenkenbali.com. We are Consulting Business and Management, especially for Foreign Investment.

Our service for retirements is Provide their legal staying permit as Visa and Kitas and provide the Tax Number.

## Channel 1

Address: Jl. Sunset Road No: 100 X, Banjar Taman - Seminyak – Kerobokan, Kuta - Bali (80361)

Telephone: 0361 7804047

Fax: 0361 730818

Website: http://www.channel1.biz/

**Can you give an overview of how to qualify for the retirement visa?**

The retirement visa is an Indonesian Semi Permanent Residential visa know as KITAS or ITAS designated for a person with minimum 55 years of age who intent to live and stay in Indonesia for a year or more. The Retirement visa is valid up to 5 years with yearly extension.

**What documents are necessary for getting the retirement visa?**

The required documents from the applicant(s) to apply for retirement visa are:

1. Copy of passport with minimum 18 months validity.
2. Statement of retirement if any.
3. Photograph 4 X 6 red background.
4. Address in the country of origin.
5. Address in Bali - Indonesia.
6. Insurance with international coverage.

**Should people apply for their visa in their home country or in Bali?**

The application can be done while the person is still in their home country. The Indonesian Government through the Immigration General will issue approval letter of the visa application called Telex visa and we will send it over the the person for him or her to obtain the visa from the Indonesian Embassy.

**How long does the whole visa application process take?**

Under normal circumstances the application should be completed after a maximum of 21 working days.

**If someone comes to Indonesia on a social visa and then they apply for the retirement visa, do they need to exit the country to pick up their visa at an Indonesian embassy overseas, like in Singapore? Or can everything be done in Indonesia?**

Yes, they must travel out of Indonesia to pick up the visa.

**Do you need a sponsor and how should people go about finding a sponsor?**

We provide the sponsorship.

**What happens if one partner is over 55 for example and qualifies for the visa and their partner is say 45 years old. What can they do about this?**

As long as they're legally married the spouse visa will be approved.

**Do people who retire in Bali have to pay tax in Indonesia on their pension?**

No, but if they travel out of Indonesia, they must pay IDR 2,500,000 fiscal tax (the fiscal tax has now been abolished).

**Should people who want to retire in Bali get an NPWP?**

Not compulsory, but some of them are having NPWP just to avoid paying the fiscal tax.

**How can people move their possessions to Bali? Can you help with that?**

They can move their personal possession after they have a KITAS or retirement visa, NOT before and the moving company will be able to assist in this matter.

**Can you tell me how much the retirement visa costs for one applicant?**

The application for this visa is IDR 7,500,000 per person for the 1st year and this not including the visa payable directly at the Indonesian Embassy which is vary from US$ 80 above depending on where the embassy is.

**How much is the cost for renewal?**

The cost of renewal is IDR 6,500,000 per person and the renewal can be done in within Indonesia, doesn't required the visa holder to travel overseas.

**What is the maximum length of time someone can stay on a retirement visa in Indonesia?**

The visa validity is 5 years; this means the person may stay up to 5 years continuously and start again from the beginning on the 6th year.

**Can you please give a brief introduction to your company and tell us about what services you provide to retired expats? How does your company differ from the many other visa agencies in Bali?**

*An information of my company can be found on our website, and we believe we provide the best service. Our company motto is: Yes we can or no we cannot, MAYBE doesn't exist.*

*We are the only agency company in Bali who is also registered under ASIC (Australian Security and Investment Commission).*

*During the past four years we have had more than 450 active clients and keep growing.*

Made in the USA
Lexington, KY
17 September 2012